Product Photography

ALL OUTSTANDING TECHNIQUES AND EQUIPMENTS FOR A
PROFESSIONAL DIGITAL PHOTOGRAPHER

By

Randy Johnson

INTRODUCTION

As technology advanced, the definition of the word career changed too. More and more job opportunities sprang up giving people the ability to either improvise or carve their own path where none existed before. Of all these mush- rooming careers, the most notable is digital photography.

What does a picture mean to you? Even in our own minds we come up with our own picture while trying to figure out things. As our fore fathers said a picture is worth a thousand words- no one yet has come up with a better way of describing our passion for capturing memories and images on film- and, in this day and age, on memory chips as well.

You may not remember most of what you see today, but you will if you record it through the lens of a camera. Unlike memories, which can shift and fade over time, photographs are unchanging images. They are a visual catalog of our lives. Moments, people, objects, and places rise from the ordinary to the significant when you capture them in photographs. With a photograph, you are telling the viewer, "This is something or someone important to me."

Cameras help us capture every moment in our life time including the people and things most dear to us — our parents, our kids, our friends, our pets. Just as you reflect on your life when viewing old pictures of yourself, so will your children use the images you create to look back on their lives. Your unknown descendants are looking over your shoulder as you record your life on film.

Cameras are also handy tools for simply documenting how things look. We use them to take pictures; of precious objects for insurance purposes, for selling items online, for documenting beginnings, middles, and ends of projects.

These images are often purely factual, without emotional content, yet they too serve an important purpose.

With the advent of digital photography in the mid 1990s, many people predicted that film-based photography would become a thing of the past, much like earlier predictions that the rise of the computer would result in the demise of the printed word. But film-based photography is very much alive (as is the printed word) and is, in fact, thriving. Not only that, the same technological advances that made digital photography possible have made film-based cameras more affordable, easier to use, and capable of doing more than they ever could before.

There are no denying digital photography's advantages over film-based shooting. At the same time, film-based photography continues to offer many advantages over digital imaging. Many photographers use both, choosing the platform that best suits their needs depending on what they're shooting. Regardless of equipment choice, knowing how to take good pictures, how to compose them, how to light them, how to capture action versus still images is still important. No amount of technological advances will at all time replace the photographer's position behind the viewfinder.

While this book is meant to provide a general overview of what photography is all about, its primary focus is on helping those photographers with passion in product photography.

These are exciting times for anyone who enjoys taking pictures. Not only are there more equipment choices and options than ever before, there are also more opportunities for sharing your work with others. Regardless of what kind of photographer you are or aspire to be, the richness of photography is so great that it can't be exhausted in a lifetime. Even the most experienced professional photographers will tell you that there is always a new challenge, something else to be learned, a technique to be honed, and a skill to be mastered. The more you use your camera, the better your life will be.

The more you take pictures, the more ways you will have to experience and savor life. Having a photographer's eye, mind, and heart will give your life deeper meaning. You will create memories and connections for years and years to come.

This is a far cry from what you would do with your fancy Smartphone camera. It is a professional arena that needs a perfect understanding of both the tools and rules of the game.

If you want to get into studio photography and learn how to take great studio photographs this book will help you. The book is designed to assist those just starting out as well as established photographers who wish to develop their lighting skills and photographic repertoire. Within these pages, you will find the relevant information needed to get you started and further develop your understanding of studio photography like a pro.

There are many different genres of photography, yet they all have one thing in common, which is to capture light.

Understanding how to make the most of light is a prerequisite for any photographer at any level in the business, the studio being no exception. As you would expect, there are some advantages to working within the studio, in that you are working within a contained environment and have full control over the light.

However, without the props and the natural background environment found on location, the studio can at times seem quite sterile, and you will inevitably need to work harder and more creatively to make the most of the shoot. This is why your understanding and application of studio lighting and photography is important.

If there is one thing that I have learned from my experience of researching for the right equipments and techniques to be incorporated in product photography it is that these photographers want clear practical advice.

I am convinced that the majority are hungry for a combination of fresh lighting ideas, the concepts behind those ideas and a greater understanding of studio terminology. Many have searched the internet and books at length without being able to find all of the necessary information in a single cohesive format, which is why I decided to write this book. No remonstrations or internet forum arguing over the smallest points; just clear and open advice that combines the lighting and photographic techniques all brought together in this book.

The advice is intended to help you understand how to get the best from your equipment and studio lighting, regardless of brand. Specific lighting examples have been set out in such a way as to enable you to understand how to light a subject, showing why it has been lit in a particular way and what type of equipment has been used. The techniques will also touch on common lighting mishaps and ways in which you can overcome them. You should find that they gradually increase in complexity as you progress your way through the book, yet remain sufficiently varied to enable you to steadily develop different ideas and apply the new skills you have mastered. Although the primary focus is on lighting techniques, other aspects of studio photography - such as equipment right through to the basics of RAW processing - are also covered. Understanding these areas helps raise both awareness and expectations.

Everybody enjoys a good photograph, and I truly believe that photography is accessible and that everybody can do it.

It is one of the few skills that can be studied at leisure. Although there are rules for good lighting, so it remains important to strike a balance between technique and creativity. Eventually, as your confidence and technical ability increase, you will begin to stamp your own personality onto your photographs. Master the techniques within these pages, build and experiment with them to create something new and different. This is what will make you a confident and well-versed photographer. Actually, this book will first introduce you to photographing; all what it takes to be an exceptional photographer and then give you all the details needed in product photography- taking pictures in studios.

Contents

CHAPTER 1

WHAT IS DIGITAL PHOTOGRAPHY

L et's go an extra mile and take a more objective approach and try understanding what digital photography is all about.

A simple definition would coin it as the taking or manipulation of photographs that are stored as digital files. You can take the picture directly by the use of a digital camera, capture a frame from a video or scan a photograph. It does not matter, provided the image you are dealing with is in digital form.

The master and primary tool of the digital world is the digital camera. It uses arrays of electronic photo detectors in order to the lens to focus of what to capture. The image is then stored on a memory card on the digital camera. It does not use the photographic film, as it was common with the prior photography. While on the memory card, the image can be transferred to a computer or any other digital device

This, in essence, creates the main separation from analogue photography and digital photography. The only way in which you could process a photographic film was by printing it.

With digital photographs, you can copy them to other storage devices, manipulate or enhance them and if possible combine a couple of images to create a mash up.

The digital photographs are represented as bit maps. While in this format, the photograph can be edited as you please.

You can add a number of effects by use of image enhancing software that we shall be looking at later on. These effects are meant to enhance its look and make it more appealing.

How the digital camera works

While digital cameras have many similar characteristics to old film cameras in that they use a lens and a combination of aperture and shutter speed to produce an exposure, what goes on inside is radically different.

Unusually in these days of ever increasing efficiency, the move from film to digital actually introduces an extra stage in the image making process. In a film camera the light entered the lens and hit the film inside. The chemicals on it reacted and the basic image was formed (it still needed to go in the developing tank but that's neither here nor there for our purposes). The film acted as both image creator and storage device.

In a digital camera the light enters the lens and strikes a computer chip known as the Charged Coupled Device (CCD) or the Complementary Metal Oxide Semiconductor (CMOS) chip. These are two similar technologies that work the same way to produce the digital image. It used to be that all DSLR cameras used CCDs because they gave sharper results, but

CMOS technology has improved significantly so that these days the fashion is to use CCD chips in compact cameras and CMOS chips in DSLRs. The CMOS chip has lower noise-that is, digital imperfections which are detailed further on, which makes it ideal for cameras where absolute quality is the prime concern.

The CCD or CMOS chip consists of rows and columns of light sensitive diodes or photosites, tightly packed together.

Light hits the diodes and is converted into a digital charge by the analogue to digital converter. The longer the shutter of the lens is left open, the more light comes in, the greater the charge in the diodes and the higher the resulting value that is recorded. This is the brightness of the image which is formed in shades of grey, from pure black to pure white.

Over the top of the CCD/CMOS sits a color filter array (CFA). There are two different types of filter available at the moment, and variations on one of them. The most common is the Bayer filter which has a mosaic pattern of green, red and blue receptors. They are arranged in a pattern so that for every four diode areas there are two green, one blue and one red receptor areas. As the light passes through the filter, it registers in the receptors and sets the color for that particular area of the image.

As you can probably guess, this means that the green sensing ability of the chip is 50% accurate and the red and blue areas are only 25% accurate. However, few colors are 100% of these primaries, so it isn't the case that there are lots of unrecorded areas. The built in computer of digital cameras analyses the spread of all the color values and fills in the gaps according to what type of image it is. This process is known as demosaicing. In this way the color element of the picture is created. The rival to the Bayer filter comes from a company called Foveon. The color filter here has three separate layers, one for each primary color. This creates more accurate color rendition as theoretically, each diode area now can now record each specific color.

So now we have a mass of digital values that represent the picture. This is the raw data and it needs to be stored somewhere. Initially it goes into an internal memory buffer, so that the CCD/CMOS can be cleared and the camera ready to take the next picture. The bigger the memory buffer, the more pictures you can shoot quickly.

From the memory buffer the image data needs to be saved into permanent memory usually a removable memory card (it can also be internal memory). The speed with which the camera can save the image from the internal buffer to the memory card dictates the overall shooting rate. A digital SLR will have a bigger buffer and faster write speeds, and so can be used to shoot more pictures, faster, than a compact camera. The exception to this is the new range of Casio high speed EXILIM compact cameras that can shoot high resolution images at DSLR speeds.

The Difference in Resolution

Compared to the film photographs, the digital photographs come with a slightly lower resolution. This is not to mean that they are of poor quality because you will hardly note the difference when placed side by side. Furthermore, the low resolution can be attributed to the fact that the digital photos are mainly used on the wild wide web. The low resolution makes it easy for everyone to see it thru internet and to download them.

The popularity of digital photography has risen fast and steady over the years. This type of photography has affected the industry in a very big way. There are as many gains as there are losses. The lose come in the form of certain complementary companies having to close shop or down size the number of workers.

It Takes a Camera and a Photographer to Make an Awesome Picture

Contrary to popular belief, a higher number of mega pixel does not out rightly equal to a great picture. It takes time, practice and dedication. When in case of latest model of digital camera and you wanted to buy it will be meaningless if you do not have the expertise to use the camera.

What this means is that it is the photographer who makes good photography and not the camera. It is not uncommon to find bad pictures taken by a state of the art camera and breath-taking photos taken by use of a mobile camera phone with less mega pixels. There are many file formats for digital photography. A good format enables compression of the files, which makes transmission on the internet faster.

During production, digital photography may be faster and cheap but it is not easy at all. Coming up with a quality product requires great expertise.

Simple Things Every Digital Photographer Must Know

A picture is worth a thousand words. This is true. What we forget to add is that a bad picture will not tell the same story as a good picture. Pictures freeze moments. How well that can be achieved depends on how well you have mastered your art.

It is all about the light

The amount of light could either make your picture great or destroy it completely. Mastering the art of balancing the light is what separates a pro from a beginner. This is the reason why most photographers will schedule their photo shoots in case there is too much sunlight. You will find majority of photographers preferring to take their photos during the early morning hours and late in the evening when the sun is setting.

Direct sunlight will always result in production of sharp shadows and it also spoils the picture. As a digital photographer, you need to understand how to position yourself in a way that the direct sunlight is no longer a hindrance. Knowing how to use the flash could make this very easy. In cases where the background is already bright, the flash helps in lighting the foreground thus eliminating the shadows.

Know your camera

There is no need of having a fancy digital camera that you hardly know anything about. Digital cameras continue to be produced by the day. There is always a new invention with every passing year. The difference is always in the features offered by the camera. These features if utilized properly will make photo shooting for you very easy.

A feature such as autofocus is invaluable once you understand how it works. It will help you do away with instances where backgrounds of picture are more profound than the subject. This and many other features may just happen to be the magic that epic pictures are made of.

Whenever you buy a new digital camera, do not just throw away the manual unless you have read and understood most of it. Ensure that you try out the instructions on the manual.

It will take some time before you finish going through the manual. Don't rush. Take your time to do it right.

Move close enough

The little details are what make up a good picture. Moving close enough to your subject will enable you to capture every single detail.

Rule of thirds

Apparently, not even the latest of technologies could write off this ancient technique. This technique entails dividing your focus area into thirds. While looking into the lens, you will then place the subject around the area where the fractions intersect. When you take the picture, everything will just turn out as it is supposed to. The background, foreground, and the object will all be perfect. This principle should serve as a guiding tool when taking your pictures but should not be used almost every single time.

Choosing Your Cameras

As we had seen earlier, a top-notch camera does not guarantee high quality pictures. Two people can possess the same camera but the resultant quality of pictures end up being very different. The camera does not shoot itself. However, it is always worth to have a good camera if you can afford it. Before making that choice there are several things that you will need to consider.

What do you need?

The world of photography is very diverse. Many photographers specialize in many different fields. With the diverse needs come different types of digital cameras to satisfy those needs. You need to know the type of photography you want to venture into. It could be product photography, landscapes, sports, or macro. The type of environment you will be operating in also matters in addition to the kind of features you want the camera to have. Lastly, your level of experience has to be considered too. You need to take time to answer the above questions if you are to get your desired type of camera.

Point and Shoot

The point and shoot camera will be the best choice if you are just a novice who is starting to explore the world of photography. It is not complicated like the DSLR and it is also affordable. The DSLR are better qualities which require proper care and maintenance. They are bigger and heavier than the point and shoot cameras. The good thing with the DSLR is that they have the largest image sensors, fast focus speeds, and wide variety of lenses. All these come at a higher price. You will also need the experience to better handle them.

The zoom and big sensor factor

As far as zooming is concerned, you will be presented with the choice of the optical or the digital zoom. Between the two, the optical zoom is a better choice as it produces better and quality pictures. The digital zoom has the inclination of enlarging the picture and making it more pixilated. The zoom ratio is significant since it determines the angle coverage of your camera. A camera that can cover wide angle shots is better especially for taking family portraits.

These three factors should help narrow down your search to a manageable number. What remains is going out to stores that sell the digital cameras and asked to test them. Eventually, you will be able to get a camera that you feel suits you best.

The flash

Having a flash on your camera is no longer a necessity. It is mandatory. Choosing detachable flash units will help you illuminate each scene appropriately before snapping the shutter. Even though most of the professional photo shoots would include backup lighting, a camera with an on board flash will always take better photos in low light areas than one without.

You however have to remember that having a flash mounted onto your camera does not mean that you should always use it. There are specific occasions when you must never use your flash. For instance, when taking photos including highly reflective surfaces, for instance mirrors or shiny surfaces, using a flash will reflect more light hence creating a 'burn' effect on the photo.

When taking close-up pictures, an active flash bulb will most likely stun the person and make them break the pose. Using secondary lighting is always advised unless you are taking paparazzi pot shots or photographing nature.

Budget

In the end, it will come down to the amount that you are ready to spend on the camera. With the wide variety, you should be able to get a good camera that is within your financial means. Spending large sums of money on a product that only differs from one that is available in terms of megapixels is not a very good idea.

Knowing Your Camera Lenses

A good DSLR (Digital single lens reflex) will push your skill and finesse beyond the limits. In essence, DSLR camera contains removable lenses meaning that you can always attach the lens you want for different pictures. The basal power of this type of a camera is in the fact that you can always take different pictures in different settings provided you have the right lens.

With this, you do not have to invest in cameras with strong lenses or impressive software processing to cover up for the changes in performance. With a DSLR, you can start simple with the cheapest lenses in the market before moving on to more expensive and impressive lenses.

So far, nothing answers the question at hand. If you can afford to invest in the compact and surprisingly effective cameras in the market that aren't DSLR but can still change lenses, then you might be good to go. Either way, you still must know how to differentiate your lenses and what to consider before buying an add-on lens.

Mount surfaces

Cameras have different mount surfaces. Most brands would love to keep their mount surfaces different from competitors meaning that there are no universal lenses unless you first use an adapter to recalibrate your mount point. Buying your brand's lens is the best way to going around this.

Focal lengths

The kind of photography you engage in should determine your lens' focal length. The focal length determines how much a camera can zoom. It also has an impact on the overall cost of the camera. For normal close up photos like model portraits, you could make do with 50mm or 75mm lenses. However, if you are into nature photographs and want to capture the beauty of that praying mantis without chasing it away, something more menacing like the 300mm lens would be perfect for the job.

DISCERNING THE CAMERAS FORMATS

Many of you reading this will already have invested in a camera or be considering purchasing one. As you know, there are many different camera systems available, some of which are more suited to studio work. There are also some less commonly known, yet extremely useful, pieces of equipment that could prove to be extremely beneficial in your work.

This is not meant to be a guide on which brand of camera you should purchase, but instead will offer some guidance as to what type of camera is more suitable for different types of studio photography, plus some advice as to what is available and some of the differences between the varying camera formats.

The Film or Digital Debate

There is always a debate about film versus digital. Both systems are not without their advocates and critics; yet both have their place in the market. Film for many years has been the accepted method of capturing images, gradually becoming less popular with the continuing development of the digital camera. Film has for the large part become a niche market and as a result acquired a certain artistic and nostalgic merit, revered and loved by many established photographers who have toiled over single images for many hours in the darkroom. It is true to say that many of the world's iconic advertising, portrait and fashion images have all been captured on film, and it is still capable of producing the same quality of image today.

For the large part, film, paper and developing technology have been left behind in favor of development of digital technology. Digital photography is accessible, quick and intuitive to use, offering instant appraisal and feedback to the photographer and as such has opened up the photographic industry to many more people. The imaging quality on offer by some of the digital systems has surpassed all quality boundaries, offering photographers huge flexibility and opportunities that would have been thought of as impossible many years ago. Whilst digital photography has never had the prestige and illusiveness of film, the sheer competitiveness of the market has raised imaging standards everywhere, pushing all boundaries of the finished photograph, from lighting to post processing.

So which suits best your path in product photography?

There is no answer to this - it is purely down to personal choice. As far as this book is concerned, the lighting techniques used will be applicable regardless of whether you use a film or digital camera system.

However, your rate of development and user experience may be enhanced more by using a digital system, as the instant feedback offered by the camera will enable you to immediately ascertain if what you are shooting looks as it should.

There are also certain markets pressures that you need to consider when investing in a system. Not just the cost of equipment, consumables and time, but also expectations from your potential client base. For example if you are planning on shooting family portraits, press photography, fashion editorial or advertising, there may well be an expectation from family, editors, producers and clients to view images both immediately and remotely. These pressures have to some degree rendered film obsolete within these markets, as this type of instant image appraisal is not possible. If you don't offer this service and somebody else does, you will undoubtedly lose business. This is why so many photographers have chosen to invest in the digital market, and film to some extent has become a more specialized medium that is used within fine-art markets.

Camera Formats

Traditionally there were four common camera formats, some deriving their names from the size of the negatives they produced. The names and the uses of the systems remained virtually unchanged even with the advent of digital capture in the late 1990s. However, manufacturers have continued to provide models to fulfill demand and gaps in the market, introducing new models that bridge the gaps between the additional formats, appealing to both professional and amateur photographers alike.

Compact Cameras

Compact cameras are small and highly portable cameras aimed at the mass consumer market. They are almost fully automated with built-in flash and fixed or non- interchangeable telezoom lenses. Film-based compacts tend to be 35mm, whereas digital systems utilize a small CCD sensor that has seen a trend of increasing pixel count with limited picture quality. Most of the digital systems offer JPEG format only images. Quality and expandability are limited, making the compact camera unsuitable for studio photography.

Bridge Cameras

Bridge cameras are a purely digital market. They are small and portable cameras offering the photographer more manual controls and longer zoom lenses than the traditional compact. Camera capabilities differ greatly from manufacturer to manufacturer. Some systems offer RAW, TIFF and JPEG image formats and higher ISO capability, whereas others may be more limited. The quality of these cameras is usually average, although they do on the whole offer quality gains over the compact cameras. Bridge cameras offer an all-in-one solution, with greater flexibility than the compact range. Depending on model, bridge cameras are either not ideal or unsuitable for studio photography.

Interchangeable Lens Compact Cameras

Interchangeable lens compact cameras offer the photographer a small portable camera system with a small choice of lenses for improved quality. They are available in both film and digital formats. The most instantly recognizable film based system is the rangefinder system, which utilizes 35mm film, and there are several digital systems to choose from. The cameras tend to employ a larger sensor than the compact and bridge markets, offering significant image quality advantages over compact and bridge camera systems. The cameras are fairly small in size (depending on lens) and are ideal for travel and street photography. Different manufactures comes up with different specifications, but most offers the photographer full manual control for creativity. Depending on specification they are suitable for studio photography, but not ideal.

35mm Based SLR/DSLR Cameras

SLR is an abbreviation for Single Lens Reflex, and DSLR is simply the digital equivalent. Most of the old film-based SLR cameras utilized 35mm film and have become less common since the introduction of the Digital SLR. There are several SLR/DSLR systems available and most have a large number of lenses available, some of which are compatible between digital and film models. The larger body of the DSLR allows some camera models to employ a larger sensor than the compact, bridge and interchangeable lens cameras, offering significant image quality advantages. DSLR systems have been designed with flexibility in mind and offer the photographer full manual and creative control of the camera. The large number of lenses and peripherals available, plus the flexibility over controlling the camera, makes SLR and DSLR systems ideal for professional studio photography.

Medium Format Cameras

Medium format has its traditional roots in the TLR (Twin Lens Reflex) cameras, such as the instantly recognizable Rolleiflex, which utilized the 120/220 roll film. As time progressed, many of these cameras developed into Single Lens Reflex systems, yet retained the use of 120/220 roll film as the larger negative of 6×6cm or 6×7cm and produced better image quality than 35mm based systems. Modern digital medium format cameras are effectively DSLR cameras that utilize a much larger sensor for significant image quality gains than those offered by the 24×35mm DSLR equivalents.

As with 35mm DSLR systems, there is a broad range of lenses and peripherals available for medium format digital systems, with some that may be compatible between films and digital. Medium format cameras come with detachable sensors, known as digital backs, similar to the film backs that housed the 120/220 roll film allowing the back to be utilized on large format systems too. Medium format cameras are renowned for extreme image quality and tonality, producing true 16-bit images, making them ideal for all genres of studio photography.

Large Format

Large format has become less common in modern photography. It was the original photographic format; long before medium format and 35mm. originally, it utilized very large negatives, more commonly 5×4in (102×127mm) but also 8×10in (200×250mm) or Ultra Large Format (ULF), offering negative size and image quality far in excess of medium format. The most recognizable large format systems are the monorail studio cameras, produced. These high-quality and precision-based cameras are ideal for product and architectural photography, utilizing an inherent tilt and shift system to facilitate the control of perspective and parallax issues. These cameras are still very much in use today by high-end professional architecture, interior and product photographers, although the film has largely been replaced by the medium format digital back, allowing the photographer to maximize the best elements of both the large format and digital systems - ideal for specific applications of studio photography.

35mm and Medium Format Technical Cameras

Recent developments have seen innovative products arrive on the market, allowing 35mm and medium format DSLRs to be mounted directly onto a technical camera based system.

Products such as the X2-Pro allow technical camera front standard movements such as rise, fall, swing, tilt and shift, affording control over perspective and focal plane issues.

This type of system is a cost effective way for all DSLR owners to obtain technical camera flexibility and prerequisites for shooting with studio Lights. Regardless of what type of camera system you intend to purchase, there are some absolute prerequisites for shooting with studio lights.

Most cameras will offer a variety of shooting modes, such as fully automatic, semi-automatic and fully manual. These will vary from manufacturer to manufacturer and depend entirely on each model, but are often known as P (program mode), Av (aperture priority), Tv (shutter priority) and M (manual).

The shooting modes you are able to use depend entirely on the type of lighting system you are employing. If you are using continuous lighting, then any of the camera's shooting modes can be used (although manual mode is preferential), as you will be able to meter the light through the camera's inbuilt TTL metering system. However, when shooting with studio flash, it becomes necessary to use the camera in fully manual mode (M) as the camera's inbuilt metering becomes redundant and is unable to meter the very short burst of flash. Studio 'flash' lighting operates completely independently to the camera's inbuilt system, so the flash needs to be metered independently and the correct ASA/ISO, shutter speed and aperture dialled into the camera system manually.

Fully automatic and semiautomatic camera modes will not work with flash- based studio lighting. If your camera does not have the option of a manual mode or manual override, then it will only be suitable for continuous lighting and not studio flash.

One other prerequisite of studio flash is that it needs to be 'triggered'.

This can be done in two ways, namely via a lead that connects to the PC Sync socket normally located on the front or side of the camera, or via a radio or infrared trigger fitted to the camera's hot shoe. The most popular method is by radio trigger, as unlike the PC Sync connector, it doesn't require a lead and offers freedom of movement up to 100 meters from the lighting equipment. PC Sync cables are the much cheaper option, but also become a hazard and are frequently tripped over or occasionally pull over the lights when the photographer attempts to stray too far! Regardless of your preferred method of triggering, it is essential that your camera has either a hot shoe or a PC Sync connector.

USING THE PC SYNC

Film cameras were originally designed to utilize the PC Sync for flash photography and may require you to set the shutter speed to a pre-defined sync mode. The most common of these settings can be found on the shutter control dial and is marked X. This is commonly known as the X- Sync and times the shutter to be completely open when the flash is at its peak illumination, thus correctly exposing the image. Depending on your camera system, you may find other settings, such as F, FP, M and ME, which were designed to be used with different types of flash bulbs, although the X setting is generally considered to be the most suitable with modern studio flash systems.

Care does need to be taken when using the PC Sync via sync cable with DSLR camera systems. Most modern studio flash systems will operate a sync voltage of less than 6 volts, whereas older flash systems may have a sync voltage well in excess of this. The specification differs depending on your camera; however, some manufacturers suggest that a PC Sync voltage in excess of 6 volts via the camera's hot shoe can cause irreparable damage.

As modern DSLRs are highly sensitive electrical devices, it is recommended that you refrain from connecting the camera via cable to the flash via the PC Sync or hot shoe without having some form of surge protection to protect your camera. There are several reports of DSLR cameras being damaged as a result of higher sync voltages of older studio flash systems, so please ensure you check with both the studio lighting and camera manufacturer to ascertain compatibility when contacting your DSLR in this way. If in doubt, always use a reputable radio trigger.

CHAPTER 2

DIFFERENT EQUIPMENTS TO CHOOSE FROM DURING PRODUCT PHOTOGRAPHY

LIGHTING

For many years, studio photography was for a large part controlled by the professional elite. However, with the introduction of digital photography, it has slowly filtered down to the semi-professional and enthusiast markets, seeing with it an increase in affordable equipment. What once was an extremely expensive investment is now available to suit every budget, from cheaper imports to high-end established brands. So what do you purchase?

As with everything, you get what you pay for, and your decision will depend on the intended use. So, if you're planning a busy high-end studio to shoot commercial campaigns on a daily basis, then budget lighting equipment won't be for you; however, if you shoot the occasional portrait or run a small business selling products online, then budget equipment might just suit your needs. Of course, it isn't always as simple as how often you shoot, but it also depends on what you are shooting; whether you need to freeze action, cover a wide area or need consistency with exposure and color. As the demands of your photography increase, so will the demands for your equipment budget.

To this end, your first major decision will be regarding the type of light you will use - namely, continuous light or flash- light. Both have their pros and cons.

Continuous Light

Continuous light is 'continuous', in that it doesn't flash - the largest and best-known continuous light source we know is the sun! However, depending on your geographic location, sunlight isn't particularly reliable, and shaping and controlling both daylight and sunlight can prove to be difficult. This is where studio lighting comes in. There is a broad range of different continuous lighting systems on the market aimed at both photographers and filmmakers.

Continuous lighting systems are intuitive to use and are utilized by both amateur and professional photographers.

They offer the benefit of visualizing the lighting levels and shadows with the naked eye, as opposed to metering each flash head with a light meter - so what you see is what you get. It has been this ease of use that has led to a growth and development by manufacturers for the enthusiast markets, meeting the demands for home portraits and small business e-commerce. Typically the continuous lights that are aimed at the amateur and beginner markets tend to be considerably cheaper than flash lighting targeted at the same level.

There are other benefits of course, such as the ease of balancing your lighting with ambient lighting levels, metering using your camera's inbuilt TTL (Through The Lens) meter instead of a handheld flash/ light meter, and depending on which continuous lighting system you're using, it may also prove easier to balance the ambient color temperature, such as daylight. However, continuous light does have its limitations and although it can be used for any subject it typically finds its niche in stills/product photography.

As you would expect, there are a number of different continuous lighting systems available; the prices can vary greatly, and each type has its strengths and weaknesses. Perhaps the most common type of continuous lighting is incandescent light, produced by the standard light bulbs found in many household lamps. As a main light source, incandescent light is particularly undesirable as it lacks power and is best described as the orange hue found on many amateur interior photographs. For this reason, many continuous lighting alternatives have been developed, including the following:

1) HID Lights (High Intensity Discharge)

HIDs are basically arc lamps that rely on a combination of gas and metal salts and an electric arc between two electrodes to produce light when ignited by current. There are various types of HID lights available to photographers, each producing a different type of light, each with a slightly different color temperature and, as you would expect, varying costs.

2) HMI Lights (Hydrargyrum Medium-arc Iodide)

Continuous lighting systems originally found their roots in the theatre with the use of incandescent hot lights, until the 1950s when a more efficient lighting system was designed by Osram-Sylvania, known as HMI lights. Instead of using incandescent light, HMI lights use arc lamps (light produced by an electrical arc inside the lamp) and are approximately four times more efficient than incandescent lights, whilst emitting less heat. HMI lights are typically expensive and can be found most frequently in theatres, broadcasting and film studios. They run at a color temperature around 5600–6000 Kelvin (standard daylight color temperature).

HMI lights are used by many photographers, especially for lighting larger subjects such as cars and interiors, and are available in wattages that are sufficient to overpower the sun.

HMI lights can be 'hot restarted', which means they can be restarted immediately after being switched off. HMI lights are traditionally known as 'Blonde' and 'Redhead' - Blonde with a power output of 1000–2000 watts and Redheads with a power output of 650–1000 watts.

3) CDM/CMH Lighting (Ceramic Discharge Metal/ Halide)

CDM lights are commonly used for architectural lighting as they produce high power, yet less heat than HMI lighting, so may be run for prolonged periods. Typically, CDM lighting produces a bluish light that is close to daylight, although the exact color temperature depends on the specific mixture of metal halide salts within the lamp. There are also warm-white CDM lamps, with somewhat warmer color temperatures, that produce a more clear and natural-looking light. There are a range of CDM bulbs available that produce color temperatures between 3000 and 8000 Kelvin. The benefits of these for photographers is that bulbs can be easily swapped to match a given color temperature. CDM lamps are said to use one fifth of the power of comparable tungsten incandescent light bulbs for the same light output and retain color stability better than most other gas discharge lamps.

CDM lights tend to be cheaper than the HMI lights; however, they are 'cold restarted', meaning they will take several minutes to warm up and will need similar downtime before they are restarted.

4) Tungsten Halogen Lights

Tungsten Halogen is incandescent lighting, utilizing a bulb with a filament of metal tungsten. Tungsten Halogen light was for many years the choice of studios for shooting stills and was used within film production, but has to some degree been superseded by flash and HMI lighting. Tungsten tends to vary on color temperature depending on manufacturer, and the bulbs produce a lot of heat, so they can prove unsuitable for work in confined spaces, close-quarter portraits and culinary photography. Tungsten lighting is very cheap and readily available; however, there have been recent reports of their public use becoming more restricted due to the health and safety requirements of many venues.

5) Cool Lights and Fluorescent Lighting

Cool lights are fluorescent lights and are typically the entry level of continuous lighting systems. They are available in a range of color temperatures, although they are usually day- light balanced between 5600 and 6000 Kelvin for photographic use. The cool lights are available as low-voltage bulbs, which are used in single lighting heads, and in the traditional fluorescent tube format, normally installed in light banks and panels. Color stability is reasonably good at around +/- 300 Kelvin. The bulbs have a very long life cycle, between 7000 and 10000 hours, and are flicker free. Florescent cool lights produce very little heat, so are ideal for portraits and stills, especially food and culinary photography.

Some manufacturers are producing tubes that can be mixed with HMI units and colored tubes specifically for lighting blue and green screens.

6) LED Lighting (Light Emitting Diode)

LED lights and panels have a similar application to that of the fluorescent cool lighting. The principle is to use high performance LED technology for improved power output, unit size and power consumption. Similar to the fluorescent tubes, they are daylight balanced, fully dimmable and flicker free. They are available in single head form, similar in appearance to the HMI lights or light panels. LED light panel, with low power consumption and low heat.

It is possible to mix continuous lighting sources. However, if the sources are all balanced to different color temperatures, you will encounter strange and somewhat distracting color shifts in your images. The only realistic way to counteract this problem would be to utilize colored gels in an attempt to equalize some of the color shifts from the differing light sources. The degree of accuracy to which you will be able to correct the color temperature will ultimately depend on the color temperature of the light source you are using and the availability of colored gels. It is worth remembering that using a colored gel will also reduce the power output of the light. Continuous lighting has many benefits, but whilst it remains a realistic option for modern photographers, especially with the video capabilities of camera systems, allowing the photographer to engage in the worlds of both moving and still images, the quality and power output of the system depend greatly on your available budget. The entry-level cool lights and light panels may prove to be more financially attractive, yet they may also be the most limiting, with the more costly and robust and higher-powered HMI units remaining beyond the reach of all but the established professional. At the budget end of the market you will find that the availability of reflectors, shapers and modifiers for continuous lighting will be limited, especially for cool lighting and light panels. These offers may prove more restrictive as your skills and needs grow.

Power is a major influencing factor when looking at continuous light sources. Light panels and cool lights produce a relatively low power output compared to flash units of the same cost, which although acceptable for smaller portraits and products, will have limitations when shooting larger subjects and a reduced ability to freeze motion because of the lack of power output. This will ultimately result in a trade-off between shutter speed, aperture and ISO/ASA. If you need to shoot a fast moving subject with a large depth of field, then you may find yourself increasing the ISO to the point that it begins to affect the quality of your images.

HMI lighting has a much greater power output than other continuous lighting; however, it also consumes a lot of energy and as a result produces a great deal of heat. Heat can be a major health and safety concern to all photographers, especially when on location, and may prove unsuitable for certain applications such as culinary photography or anything where the heat may affect the product being photographed. Heat output can also affect portraits and model based shoots within confined, non- air-conditioned spaces or over prolonged periods, rendering them very uncomfortable, with the added issue of bright continuous light causing the subject's iris to close down and pinpoint.

Finally, most continuous light sources, such as HMI and tungsten, have a finite lifespan and after time the color temperature will begin to vary. Cheaper CDM units have the added issue of warming up and cooling down before they achieve the correct color temperature. It is the combination of power output, heat, size and flexibility that leads to continuous lighting being most frequently and commonly used for products, automotive, video, theatre and broadcasting. Many of these systems may also require high-powered, three-phase power supplies, which are not generally available in your average home.

Flash Lighting

Flash lighting is by far the most popular choice for studio photographers. It is available in three different formats - on-camera/pop-up flash, flash guns (or Speedlites) and studio flash (normally monobloc or generator based) - which normally have three very different uses. Every system is different in terms of design, use, flexibility and power output.

1) On-camera/Popup Flash

On-camera/popup flash is without a doubt the most instantly recognizable and widely available type of flash on the market. It is exactly what it says it is, and that is flash that is built into the camera or flash that pops up out of the camera when needed. Generally it is very small and highly portable, but has a very low power output and is fixed to the camera. It is most often found on compact cameras, entry-level DSLRs and occasionally some high-end DSLRs and is usually automatically controlled by the camera by way of program settings and in-camera metering. It produces a very flat, bright and unflattering light when used as the main light source, although it can be useful as fill-flash in bright sunlight or high-contrast scenes. As it is fixed, it lacks the flexibility of either hot shoe/flash guns or studio flash. Overall, it has limited professional use.

2) Flash Guns/Speedlites

Flashguns (also known as hot shoe flash or Speedlites) are separate flash units that can be placed directly onto the hot shoe of the camera or off-camera by way of a cable between the camera and the flash, or infrared. Flashguns vary in size from manufacturer to manufacturer, produce considerably more power than on-camera flash and are generally battery operated. The more expensive models can be tilted and rotated, so that the light may be bounced off ceilings, walls and through diffusers, making the light more flattering than direct flash. Press, wedding, event and social photographers frequently use flash guns as they are highly portable and can be easily controlled by way of the camera's bespoke metering system, or with standard TTL (Through The Lens) metering.

Flash guns tend to be produced by individual camera manufacturers and are usually tailored to work with their own cameras and metering systems, although there are several third-party flash gun manufacturers that will produce systems designed to make the most of individual features offered by particular camera brands and models.

Some bespoke flash systems will allow photographers to achieve extremely high sync/shutter speeds that are not always available with studio-based flash systems. It is also possible to use several flash guns together to create different lighting effects; although the caveat is that new models are introduced by manufacturers every couple of years, and backwards compatibility may at times be an issue - generally not a problem with studio flash.

Although flash guns are cheaper to purchase than studio flash units and are extremely portable, they can prove to be somewhat limited when it comes to power output, color accuracy and flexibility when shaping and controlling light.

3) Studio Lights/Studio Flash (also known as strobe lighting)

Studio lights offer more power and creative flexibility than flash guns and on-camera flash. There are many different brands, but three general types of studio light are available and their names particularly relate to their design and the way in which they are powered and operated, namely monobloc, generator operated or battery-powered. With the exception of battery power, studio heads are generally mains operated or can be linked to three-phase systems in bigger commercial studios.

Monoblocs/Monolights

Monoblocs are the most common and most popular studio light available as not only are they usually the cheapest to purchase, but they also offer a great deal of expandability and flexibility for the photographer. Monoblocs are an all- in- one design, meaning that the power supply, controls and flash are built into a single head unit. Because of this, they are generally larger in size than the heads controlled by a generator and vary hugely in power output depending on brand, anywhere from 150W to 1500W. The greater the power output, the larger the size (and heavier the weight) of the monobloc. Monobloc studio head, with controls and power supply all integrated with a single light.

Monoblocs have the flexibility of being able to be plugged directly into the mains electricity supply, placed independently of other monobloc heads providing there is a suitable power outlet nearby. When you need to adjust the power of the monobloc, it is simply a case of adjusting the controls on the head itself, which is very convenient, unless the monobloc is placed somewhere that is not so accessible.

Studio Generators

Generators (also known as packs or studio packs) can usually power up to four studio heads (depending on model).

The studio heads (or pack heads) are different in design to the monoblocs, as all the power and the controls for the head are found within the generator. The generator head will usually consist of just the flash bulb and a modeling light and on/off switch. A thick cable will connect the head directly to the generator that controls all the functions. Generators can offer many advantages over monobloc heads, such as power, recycling time, shorter flash durations and greater color consistency, but they also demand a much greater price.

As with monoblocs, generators usually plug directly into the mains power supply; however, the positioning of the heads can be limited to the length of the cable between the head and the generator (extender cables are generally available from the main lighting manufacturers). Apart from performance advantages, generators allow photographers to adjust the power of their heads on the generator itself, reducing the need to climb on chairs and ladders to access controls on the heads as with monobloc heads. There is an obvious convenience benefit to this design, especially when heads are placed so that they may not be as accessible.

As a rule, generators will afford the photographer greater control over the distribution of power between the heads connected to it, either symmetrically or asymmetrically. So for example, if a generator has two channels, symmetrical power delivery will split the power distribution 50/50 across both channels, whereas asymmetrical power distribution would allow the user to, say, direct two-thirds of the power to one channel and the remaining third to the other. As generators can offer anywhere between 1500W and 5000W of power, it helps if you can divide the power output between the heads (or channels), to allow greater control over the power delivery, as there are many occasions when minimum power is more important than maximum power.

Battery Generators

The battery generator is essentially a generator that runs from a battery power source. Some battery generators will also run from the mains and can be used in the same way as a normal AC-powered generator. As it is a generator, all of the controls to regulate the power output and modeling facility and so on will be operated from a control panel located on the pack itself and not on the heads. You will usually find that the studio-based generators and battery generators made by the same manufacturers will use the same heads and remain fully compatible. Some battery generators also offer a DC power source to operate battery-controlled monobloc heads. Battery generators are normally fairly expensive, but they offer more power and faster recycle times between flashes, plus the added flexibility of their use on location.

Battery Packs

Battery packs differ from battery generators as they offer only a power supply and basic interface, usually to a monobloc style head. As they are designed to provide DC power to monoblocs, all of the lighting functions are operated using the existing controls built into the monoblocs. On the whole, battery packs are smaller and cheaper than generators, and may also offer hot swappable battery systems to facilitate your shooting time whilst on location. The caveat is that they do not always offer a modeling light facility; they recycle slower than a battery generator and will require you to carry around larger monobloc heads.

Ringflash

Classic Ringflash is typically an expensive generator- based flash that is shaped into a ring. The camera's lens is then pushed through the centre of the ring. It produces a very flat light as it is located directly on the camera axis. Ringflash was originally designed many years ago for dental photography, but became popular with fashion photographers, producing a continuous shadow/halo around the edge of the subject, yet it is equally useful as a fill light, evenly filling the shadows or even off-axis. The recent surge in popularity has seen more affordable products arrive on the market, such as battery-powered Ringflash systems for macro photography and even adapters to convert standard studio heads into a temporary Ringflash.

Generally, photographers that are just starting out will make their first investment in monoblocs/monolights, simply because they offer extremely good value for money and a lot of flexibility. It is normally possible to purchase several monoblocs for the same price as a single generator, meaning that it is possible to quickly add heads and peripherals as your lighting develops. The difficulty is choosing the most suitable lighting manufacturer to invest your hard-earned cash in, as switching brands later on can prove expensive.

Most lighting manufacturers aim to produce a complete and compatible lighting system that can be expanded as the photographer's skills and business grow. They normally produce an extensive range of quality peripherals, soft boxes, shapers and modifiers compatible with their system. The more established the manufacturer, the more shaping tools and peripherals they will offer and the more available and widely distributed they will be. For this reason, it is important to think ahead when purchasing your first system as cheaper equipment can often prove to be more expensive in the long run. It is worth considering that established brands are established for a reason, usually because they offer good service, continuous product development and a reliable product. To this aim, it is recommended that you think long term and purchase a quality item, one that offers service in your country and the flexibility to expand the system, as opposed to purchasing the cheapest product available.

The basic prerequisites of all studio lights are very similar and have been for many years, in that they all have modeling lights, slave cells and dials to control the power output. To this extent, they will usually all work together, regardless of brand.

There are many professionals that use more than one brand of lighting, depending on the type of work they are doing, whether it may be location or studio, continuous lighting or flash. Some photographers may use more than one brand, but tend to use them within different areas of their work; whereas other photographers that have invested heavily in a particular product may purchase one or two lights from a different manufacturer to make the most of a unique quality or a particular modifier.

You will find that each lighting manufacturer's specifications will be different, and for the most part it should not be an issue with standard product shoots or portrait sessions. However, depending on how far you push the boundaries of your equipment, issues may begin to appear, such flash duration, color temperature consistency and flash recycle time. Specifications aside, the main issue will undoubtedly come with the use and exchangeability of modifiers, shapers and soft boxes. All of the established lighting manufacturers use their own mounting system - that is, the system used to attach modifiers and soft boxes to the flash heads. Using lights from several different manufacturers will mean that you may not have the freedom to exchange modifiers and soft boxes freely between your lights, limiting the flexibility of your equipment. Currently, the most common mounting system available for flash lighting is the S-type

Bayonet mount that was originally designed by the UK manufacturers. A patent loophole has seen this mounting system adopted by several lighting manufacturers, resulting in a large number of available reflectors and modifiers.

Hiring equipment is not cheap by any means; however, it is a more cost-effective way in which you can try particular brands and pieces of equipment in your own time, without the added pressure of a salesman standing over you. If you are genuinely at a crossroads in making a decision, then hiring will be the best way to make an informed choice. It is also ideal for that one-off project where you may need a specialty or expensive item, allowing you to make use of the equipment at a fraction of the cost of the original purchase (and storage). Most hire charges are tax deductible and you will be required to register your details with the hire company prior to hiring. Remember to factor in insurance/damage waiver charges, plus delivery and return days into the total number of days hire.

Flash Duration

Flash duration - the time it takes for a flash to peak and trough - is important to many professional photographers.

To the human eye, flash duration is indistinguishable from one system to another; however, it is vitally important to understand how and when you can use it. It may even influence your choice of lighting system.

For many photographers, especially those photographing static products or subdued portraits, flash duration is not an issue. This all changes from the point at which you wish to freeze motion such as splashing water or moving hair. In this scenario, the shorter the flash duration, the less motion blur you will get. It is a difficult concept for many newer studio photographers to grasp at first as most assume that any flash head will freeze everything, because they are still in the mind set of photographing in ambient light where they were wholly reliant on shutter speed to freeze subjects. However, in the studio, where most cameras are limited to a sync speed of 1/125-1/200sec it is flash duration that is king.

LENSES AND FILTERS

A lens is basically an optical device that transmits and refracts light. As to how well it does this depends entirely on the lens, the accuracy of the engineering and the quality of the optics inside. Lens design and manufacturing is an exact and highly complex science. For the most part, it is not something that a photographer needs to worry about, other than knowing the types of lenses available and which models are generally 'good' or 'bad'.

Types of Lens

Prime Lenses

Prime lenses are fixed lenses. This means they only have one focal length (unifocal), which is fixed. As a general rule, prime lenses are usually of superior optical quality than zoom lenses, as their construction is much simpler and they have fewer moving parts. The prime lens can be accurately tuned to one focal length, rather than making the best of several focal lengths, so it generally produces a sharper image than a zoom lens. As they require fewer optics, prime lenses often achieve a much wider aperture, allowing a shallower depth of field and greater flexibility when shooting in low light, with apertures as wide as f1.2. Zooming is not possible with a prime lens, meaning that the photographer has to physically move nearer or further from the subject.

Zoom Lenses

Zoom lenses allow the photographer to alter the focal length of the lens, zooming in and out from the subject, without having to move physically from their current location. Zoom lenses tend to consist of a number of different optics inside the body, some of which slide backwards and forwards as the lens is physically zoomed in and out. They are known as either par focal, meaning that they retain the focus on the subject whilst being zoomed, or varifocal, which means that the focus is lost when the lens is zoomed and the photographer will need to refocus.

Zoom lenses offer maximum convenience for photographers, allowing them to get close to a subject and flatten perspective when they need to. However, they tend not to be as consistently sharp as prime lenses and will often have a 'sweet spot', where the lens is at its sharpest at a given focal length and aperture. Given the number of optics within the zoom lens, they tend to be fairly bulky compared to a prime lens and will only offer maximum apertures of around f2.8, even in the most expensive lenses.

Telephoto Lenses

A telephoto lens is a long-focus lens where the physical length of the lens is shorter than the prescribed focal length, so for example, where the focal length of a lens is 300mm but the physical length of the lens body is shorter than 300mm. Telephoto lenses incorporate a group of lenses, known as a telephoto group, which effectively extends the light path, creating a long-focus lens that can be fitted into a much shorter lens body. They can be zoom or prime lenses and are usually defined and put into groups depending on their focal length. As a rough guide, a short telephoto will have a focal length of around 60-100mm, medium telephoto 135-300mm and super telephoto 300+mm.

Wide-angle Lenses

Wide-angle lenses are lenses that offer a much shorter focal length than a standard 50mm lens, normally 35mm and less.

Whilst a telephoto lens will compress the image perspective and offer a shallow depth of field, a wide-angle lens will increase the appearance of distance and offer a greater depth of field. Wide-angle lenses are most commonly used in architectural photography, landscapes and interiors. They tend to distort perspectives, causing parallel lines to converge and on occasions barrel distortion. Some lenses are available with focal lengths of less than 10mm, which are most commonly known as fisheye lenses.

The choice of lens is a very personal one. It can be based on several factors including subject matter, focal length, sharpness, personal preference or even budget.

Tilt and Shift Lenses

Tilt and shift lenses are essentially based upon a similar idea to the large format based camera system that operates using the Scheimpflug principle, allowing asymmetric tilts and swings to bring the subject plane, lens plane and sensor plane to meet at a virtual point (Scheimpflug intersection).

What this means is that the lens can be tilted, allowing the photographer to correct converging lines and perspective associated issues. Manufacturer specific tilt and shift lenses available for SLR and DSLR systems are portable prime lenses mounted on a tilting and shifting lens body affording some control over perspective. Tilt and shift lenses are commonly used in studio product photography, interiors and architectural photography.

Macro Lenses

Macro lenses are primarily designed for macro photography, also known as close-up photography. You will probably have seen many incredible macro images of plants and insects that allow you to see every minute hair and detail. These are shot with macro lenses and they allow the photographer to focus very closely on their subject.

Traditionally, macro lenses look similar to a short telephoto lens and will focus within a few centimeters of the subject. They are specifically optimized for high reproduction ratios, usually 1:1 or 1:2, and their use normally depends on the focal length of the lens. Shorter focal lengths will be used for stills and product photography, whereas the longer focal lengths will be more useful for insects and applications where it is not possible for the photographer to get close to the subject without disturbance.

Macro lenses can be used in the same way as any other lens, and their excellent optics produce very sharp results, which makes them suitable for both portraits and products.

Which lens to choose?

The choice of lens is a very personal one. Many photographers swear by certain lenses and have used them for so long, they know exactly how to predict the results. Certain genres of photography have specific lenses that are more widely regarded as suitable for studio work, whether it is portrait, fashion or beauty.

It is widely accepted that a good starting point for portrait shooting would be a focal length between 85mm and 150mm (35mm equivalent). Remember that the longer the focal length, the flatter the perspective and the tighter the crop on your subject. Not only does a longer focal length help flatten the perspective, but it also tends to be more flattering for the subject. In contrast a wide-angle lens would require you to get closer to your subject, distorting the perspective and making your subject look larger - and very few people want to be larger in a photograph! Generally, 85mm is the standard, moving into 100mm and 150mm for half-length and headshots respectively.

Another consideration is the size of your studio or the dimensions of the space you are working in. If you are going to be shooting within a confined space or small home studio, then a 130mm lens may well prove to be too long, as you will be unable to step far enough away from your subject when you need to fit more of them in the frame; whereas with an 85mm, you will have a wider field of view, yet it will still be possible to move closer for a tighter crop when needed. The zoom lens has brought about a handy solution and is very popular with studio photographers. Essentially, the zoom lens does all of the work of moving in and out, allowing the photographer to remain in the same position if necessary. For the most part, studio portraits are shot between f8 and f16, and zoom lenses stopped down to this aperture will still prove to be fairly sharp.

It is important to stress that there are no rules, and experimentation with shorter focal length lenses can lead to some very interesting shots; however, unless you are shooting large groups, focal lengths wider than 50mm tend to distort perspectives, creating barrel distortion, which is not very flattering to the subject and will offer little control over the depth of field. It is worth considering the important factor about depth of field, as not all portrait and fashion work is photographed within a studio environment. The longer the focal length and wider the aperture, the shallower the depth of field and the more you will be able to blur the background.

A blurred and out-of-focus background is often desirable for studio portraits, helping to provide separation between it and your subject.

All lenses will render light differently, and you would be forgiven for thinking that the most important part of the image is the sharp details of your subject; however, even the out-of-focus areas of your photograph are important and will be affected by the type and quality of lens you are using.

Many portrait photographers prefer to have sharp subjects and blurred backgrounds, because it places the emphasis on the subject. Bokeh is the term used to describe the out-of- focus areas of your image. Good bokeh would ideally be described as a milky and undefined background, whereas poor bokeh would have defined edges. Some lenses actually have a defocus control, allowing the photographer to manipulate spherical aberration and improve the bokeh.

As for your choice of lenses a selection of prime lenses (50mm, 85mm, 100mm and 130mm) are a good start, allowing working in different studio environments. Alternatively, a smaller selection of zoom lenses, such as 24–70mm and 70–200mm, will prove to be worthy alternatives.

When selecting lenses for product photography this depends on the product; the true purpose of the photograph is usually to capture a product in the best and most appealing way possible. As a rule, it needs to be accurate, as the intended market will need a clear representation of what is being sold. For some products, say those that have been engineered, the photograph will need to be a clear and scaled representation, whereas other products, such as cosmetics or food, may rely on the photograph being more representative of a lifestyle.

As a whole, the product needs to be seen in its best light and without distortion, so you will find, as with portraits, lenses with a longer focal length tend to be most suitable. Of course, products can be anything from cars to computer processors, so each subject will require its own approach and its own lens considerations.

As a standard for tabletop products, anything from 80mm would be suitable. It is worth remembering that the longer the focal length of the lens, the shallower the depth of field, which is an important consideration should you need to photograph an arrangement of products and keep them all in focus. The addition of a good quality macro lens is also a worthwhile investment, allowing high-quality close-up shots of product details.

Although more costly, tilt and shift lenses and large format camera systems are used frequently in product photography due to their ability to correct parallax and perspective issues, and this can open up a whole new world of lenses. It is not only medium format systems that can be used with this type of system as there are third-party products, from reputable studio equipment manufacturers, that will allow many DSLRs to be connected to a set of tilt and slide bellows, which may be adapted to take many of the precision lenses used on the large format system.

It is worth keeping an open mind with product photography, whilst considering the effects that certain lenses will have in terms of distortion and depth of field.

Lens Filters and Bellows

A lens filter is basically an optical filter that is placed on the front of your lens. They are available in a variety of different systems from several manufacturers; the most recognizable being the screw-in filter, available in different diameter sizes from 30.5mm to 127mm, depending on the size of the lens they are intended for. The ø symbol is normally followed by the filter diameter, for example ø49mm. There are several plastic filter systems available, which comprise of small Perspex sheets made to slide into a filter holder that is attached to the front of your lens.

It is easy to forget about the importance of lens filters now that most of us are in the digital age. For film users, lens filters are still very much a necessary part of the photographic kit, whereas many digital photographers have resorted to the use of post-processing techniques to correct issues. Post-processing may work fine as part of your work- flow for the occasional photograph, but may prove to be highly inefficient when you have shot several hundred images. It is safe to say that regardless of your photographic genre, it is important to get the exposure, composition and color balance as accurate as possible 'in camera', and this is where lens filters may help you achieve that.

Polarizing Filters

There are two types of polarizing filter: linear and circular.

Circular polarizers- are the most common, as they do not interfere with the camera's inbuilt metering system. Polarizing filters are as useful with digital photography as they are with film and they can be used regardless of whether you are shooting in black and white or color. Polarizers do not alter the color balance of the photograph, but instead filter light that has a certain direction of polarization, such as distracting reflections in glass or shiny surfaces. They also help saturate the colors of the image and are useful for darkening skies in landscape photography.

Clear, UV (Ultraviolet) and Skylight Filters

There is a difference between clear filters and UV filters, although in practice they are used in the same way. A clear lens is a 'flat' lens, in that it filters no light. Its main purpose is to protect the front element of the lens from unwanted marks and scratches - a worthwhile investment for expensive lenses. A UV filter is often used in the same way as a clear filter. It is different from the clear lens as it does actually filter out UV light. Ultraviolet light is invisible to the human eye but visible to film and digital camera sensors. The effects of UV filters are fairly neutral and as such they can remain on the front of your lens indefinitely, especially in the studio, as most studio lights have UV coated flash tubes. The effects are more obvious when shooting outside, where they help filter out the haziness caused by UV light.

Skylight filters are commonly mistaken for UV filters and have no real place within a studio environment. They are most commonly used with film and when shooting out- doors, their purpose being to remove the bluish tint often found when shooting on color film during the day, thus improving the color accuracy and warming up the photo- graph.

Color Correction Filters

Color correction filters are most commonly used by those photographers that shoot on film. They have several uses, such as correcting color casts from various lighting sources such as tungsten or adding colored effects to photographs. Their use is not restricted to colored film however; they have an important role to play in black and white photography for contrast enhancement, where colors such as yellow help darken skies and foliage. There is no universal system for naming colored filters, although some manufacturers make use of Wratten numbers, a system introduced by Kodak, for example: CC30R (CC meaning color correction, 30 indicating the strength of the filter and R for the color; in this case red). On the whole, most manufacturers will produce a series of filters, each one graded in relation to the last.

The effects produced by colored filters can often be reproduced fairly quickly in digital photography, so they are seldom used within a color temperature managed studio environment.

Neutral Density (ND) Filters

There are two types of ND filters: the solid ND and the graduated ND filter. A solid neutral density filter helps to equally attenuate (block out) light of all colors. It is most frequently used in landscapes to facilitate a longer exposure in natural daylight, where the lighting cannot be controlled. A graduated neutral density filter will attenuate light at different points on the filter. The most common graduated ND filter is where the filter is darker on one side. This is useful for controlling bright areas of the photograph, such as skies, to maintain a more consistent exposure across the frame. They are not in common use within the photo studio where the lighting can be consistently controlled; however, they may prove useful when shooting outdoors or on location.

Diffusion/Softening filters

The diffusion lens is popular with portrait photographers as it softens subjects and gives the image a more traditional 'hazy' effect. To some extent, these lenses have been replaced by the capabilities of modern software, which can recreate the effect; this requires more post-processing but affords you the option of removing the effect. Too much computerized blur tends to blow highlighted areas of the photograph, leading to unsightly white blurred masses, and for this reason some photographers prefer to use a diffusion filter to create a more precise and genuine effect.

Close-up filters/Extension Bellows/ Teleconverters

The close-up filter is essentially a converging magnifying lens built into a screw-in filter housing, so it is not technically a filter. It works in a similar way to a lens found in a pair of glasses which has been placed in front of the camera's lens to magnify the subject further. Close-up lenses come in a variety of different magnifications, such as +1, +2, +3 and so on, and can be stacked (used together) to increase their magnification further. The intended market is a cost-effective alternative to the macro lens, although the optical quality is not comparable.

A cheaper alternative would be bellows, and if you have worked within a darkroom bellows will be instantly recognizable. On 35mm SLR format camera systems, an extension bellows is intended to work in the same way as the darkroom enlarger. The pleated bellows are attached to the lens mount of the camera and allow the lens to be attached to the opposing end. The bellows then allow the lens to be moved back and forth along a rail, creating an extension of dark space between the lens and sensor/film. The net result of this is increased magnification. Bellows were originally designed for manual focus 35mm film cameras and as such have no metering or autofocus capabilities, and as they make the viewfinder significantly dimmer, focusing may become more difficult, especially in the smaller viewfinders found in modern DSLRs. Manual metering needs to be compensated for by several f stops (depth of field).

The modern DSLR equivalent to extension bellows/ extension tubes are otherwise known as Teleconverters. The benefits are that they allow autofocus and metering. The principle is the same, in that spacer 'tubes' are added between the lens and camera body. In the same way close-up lenses can be stacked and additional tubes can be added to further increase the magnification. The more tubes you add, the less light gets to the sensor/film, so if you are manually metering, you will need to adjust the camera's settings accordingly to allow for the reduction in light (usually by 'stopping up').

All of these systems are suitable for studio product photography, especially when photographing smaller products.

Always take into consideration that the longer the focal length and the closer you get to your subject, the shorter the depth of field.

CHAPTER 3

GENERAL STUDIO EQUIPMENT

Studio Stands and Tripods

S tudio stands and tripods are key pieces of equipment when shooting in the studio, more so when shooting products.

They are less commonly used when shooting portraits and other model based studio work, as the subject and the photographs tend to be more dynamic, so the photographer cannot always afford to be rooted to one particular spot with a tripod. As to whether you need to use a tripod or studio stand, this will to some degree depend on what you are shooting and the camera system you are using. Products are fairly static, and there are times when it is important to remain consistent with height and angle when shooting a series of products, which is where a support of some description lends itself.

So what are the differences between a studio stand and a tripod? Studio stands are not designed to be very portable.

They are large and heavy articulated stands that glide around on wheels within the professional studio. The arms and joints of the stand are usually designed for precision positioning and engineered with ball bearing and hydraulic joints. They are ideal for large format and heavy camera systems, where small and precise movements are necessary, and they have enough weight to allow cameras to be placed directly above products, like with a boom arm.

Lighting stands and Clamps

Lighting stands are the stands that support your studio lights. There are several different brands and types available, designed for different uses. The most common lighting stand is the type normally supplied with lighting kits. They are a lightweight extending tubular design that fold away for maximum portability and have been adapted for several different purposes, such as backlight stands and floor stands.

For the majority of photographers and day-to-day shooting, these stands are perfectly adequate and ideal for smaller heads, small-to- medium-sized soft boxes and parabolic.

There are times when heavier support stands are needed, especially when using heavy lighting heads as big modifiers.

For this, Century Stands (most commonly known as C- Stands) produced by several companies, are more adept at taking weight, as they are fitted with counter-balances and their legs partially buried in soft earth or sand. Century stands are heavier and more expensive than the standard tubular stands, so are able to support more weight at a greater height, without bowing or flexing.

Boom arms and boom stands are essentially lighting stands with an extending arm that can be rotated at an angle.

A studio head is placed at one end of the extending arm and a counterbalance at the other. They allow photographers to place lights and other equipment directly above subjects without the stand straying into the camera frame. Booms are available in several forms, from small extending arms that can be attached to lightweight stand right through to purpose-built, heavy-duty, and fully articulated gear-operated stands.

A boom is an essential piece of equipment for people and product photographers, and consideration should be given to the weight of heads and modifiers in use before purchasing. Boom arms that are not strong enough to support the weight of the equipment in use will fail with fairly catastrophic consequences.

As you would expect, to accompany the stands there are a range of clamps. These are most utilized in the professional studio, frequently by product photographers to support products, lighting and props in specific positions. Clamps are available in different sizes and designs for many different applications from joining overhead lighting support systems to clamping background paper. It is generally recommended for all photographers to carry several small grips and clamps in their kit bag, including people photographers, as they have many uses, such as clipping together baggy clothing on models and attaching colored gels to studio lights.

Tethered shooting

Tethered shooting is still a mystery to many digital photographers, yet once they have utilized it, they rarely want to return to using the camera's LCD. All photographers have shot directly to card or directly to film, depending on whether they are shooting digital or film. It is flexible, portable and very quick.

Tethered shooting is just as quick, although slightly less portable, as the camera is connected (tethered) directly to the computer or laptop via USB or Fire wire cable. The camera's functions can be controlled either on the camera or via the software, and a storage card is no longer necessary as all images are stored directly onto the computer's hard drive.

The great benefit is that you get a much larger image on the computer screen than you do on the camera's LCD, enabling you to see much more detail in the images as you are shooting, plus it can be useful for checking the accuracy of the white balance and exposure when using a calibrated system.

For product photography and high-end medium format camera systems, tethered shooting is a must. It reduces the need for the photographer to constantly strain to look down the viewfinder when the camera is placed in an awkward position and to constantly change media card. Focusing, camera settings and storage can all be done conveniently via the software on the computer.

Soft box

As the name suggests a soft box is essentially a box that produces soft light. Soft boxes come in many different sizes and shapes, with the shape of the box forming part of the name, such as Octabox (eight sides), Hex box (six sides) and Strip- box (thin soft box). The box is erected using flexible rods that shape the covering (reflective on the inside and black on the outside). Once constructed, a white nylon diffuser is fixed to the open aperture of the box to soften the light. The most common type of soft box fits directly to the front of the studio head, allowing the light to pass directly out of the front diffuser. More expensive models allow heads to be inverted within the box, allowing the light to bounce off the internal surfaces before travelling out of the diffuser, thus creating a flatter and more even light. Soft boxes have a broad range of uses and afford more control over the light. They are often used for portraits but less so for professional beauty work due to the square shape and catch light.

Beauty Dish

Beauty dishes come in several sizes and are ideal for single portraits and beauty style photographs. The dishes are equipped with a centralized diffuser built into the dish. The diffuser bounces the direct light back into the bowl of the reflector, helping to reduce proximity hot spots and create a softer light that is more flattering. They occasionally come with additional diffusers and 'shower-caps' to further soften the light. Beauty dishes are favored by beauty photographers, as the round reflector is more flattering to the shape of the face when in broad lighting. They produce a slightly harder and more defined light than a soft box.

Narrow Reflectors (Snoots): 10–20 Degree Spread

Reflectors this narrow are usually in the form of snoots. These are cone-shaped to deliver a controlled spot of light. Snoots create defined hard shadows and can be coupled with honeycomb grids to concentrate the light further, lighting small areas.

Directional Reflectors: 25-50 Degree Spread

A directional reflector is designed to project the light forwards and usually take on more of a parabolic shape. The longer and narrower the reflector, the tighter and more directional the light will be. Their use is varied and will depend on how much control is needed over the light and the amount of power you want to place in a particular area. When used as key lights, they tend to produce long, well-defined shadows with high contrast. The coverage will depend entirely on the size of the reflector. Many photographers find them useful for projecting light and maximizing output. They can also be useful for lighting specific areas with honeycomb grids and background scenery/paper. As with all reflectors, the internal coating will directly affect the intensity of the light.

Standard Reflectors: 50-60 Degree Spread

Medium-angled reflectors sit in between wide-angled reflectors and directional reflectors. They create a medium amount of spread of light and can be used in a wide variety of lighting situations. They are normally shorter and broader in design than directional reflectors and less open than wide- angled reflectors. They are particularly useful when fitted with honeycomb grids and barn doors to help control and direct the light in specific areas. As with all reflectors, the internal coating will directly affect the intensity of the light.

Medium to Wide-Angle Reflector: 60–70 Degree Spread

There is no absolute definition of a medium to wide-angle reflector as it depends entirely on each individual manufacturer and how they classify them. Some manufacturers classify 65 degrees as a standard reflector, whilst others will market them as medium to wide-angle. They basically spread the light more than a standard reflector and are used to cover a larger area. They can be superlative for replicating sunlight when placed at a distance or for using with gels to color a broad area. The internal coating will directly affect the intensity of the light. As with standard reflectors, they are particularly effective when used with honeycomb grids and barn doors to control the light.

Wide-Angle Reflector: 70+ Degrees

The wide-angle reflector allows the light to cover a larger area. The most common use is larger beauty dishes and umbrella reflectors. They are usually shallow in depth, allowing the light to spread out quickly. Wide-angled reflectors may also prove useful for bouncing light off surfaces within smaller environments. Surfaces for umbrella reflectors are normally glossy to maximize light output, whereas beauty dishes are coated to help diffuse the light.

Honeycomb Grids

Honeycomb grids are perfect for controlling the direction of the light, increasing contrast and shadow definition; the larger the honeycomb, the wider the spread of light and vice versa. They do not have universal fittings and are designed to fit specific reflectors, simply push-fitting or clipping into the front of the reflector. Honeycomb grids have a broad range of uses and are particularly useful when utilizing several different light sources to highlight different areas.

Egg Crates

Egg crates are for use with soft boxes. They fit into the front of the soft box over the diffuser panel. Their job is similar to that of the honeycomb grid, in that they are there to help restrict the spread of the light, giving you more directional control and fewer spills, whilst still maintaining a soft light. Egg crates are usually designed to fit specific soft boxes and are not necessarily a universal fit.

Fresnel Lens

The Fresnel lens (pronounced Fraynel) is similar to that seen in a lighthouse. It consists of a series of concentric angular sections to focus the light. Apart from lighthouses, the Fresnel lens has been made instantly recognizable by the use of HMI stage lighting and Hollywood-style lighting.

Many lenses include a built-in iris to help narrow the beam of light and produce a central spot effect with defined shadows, with a gently feathered outward gradient. The Fresnel is ideal for portrait and fashion photography, offering a large amount of control over the spread of the light.

Spotlights/Attachments

A spotlight produces a defined spot of light. It is different to the snoot because the light is projected through a series of lenses, allowing the photographer to focus and defocus the spot, intensifying or softening the shadow edges. The focus light also allows them to be used with gobos, masks and patterns to project shapes. Spot attachments with multiple lenses may be adjusted to change the spread of the light.

Barndoors

Barndoors are useful pieces of studio equipment. They fit onto the front of various reflectors and allow the photographer to flag the light, helping to control unwanted spill.

The doors may be moved to increase or reduce the amount of light spilling onto other parts of the set. They are particularly handy when controlling gelled lights.

Barndoors: ideal for flagging light and reducing unwanted spill.

ADDITIONAL USEFUL TOOLS AND EQUIPMENTS USEFUL EQUIPMENT

You might assume that a set of good quality studio lights, a decent camera and a studio table are all you need to capture studio-based still life photographs. There is a lot you can do of course with this basic equipment, but most professional product and still life photographers will use a variety of different items and tools to get results. It is not simply a case of placing items onto the table; the skill comes in positioning them exactly where you want them, at the right height and the right angles. This will not only ensure that the light is right and consistent, but will potentially save you hours of Photoshop. You still need Photoshop, but with the right techniques you can reduce the time you spend behind the computer.

The good news is that many of these items are fairly cheap and widely available from various stores or photographic retailers.

Common Accessories

Sticky Tape

Tape is useful in many ways, in particular double-sided tape and duck tape. It is ideal for sticking objects together, suspending and stabilizing things. There are other specialized tapes that do not leave any residue, which can also be very useful on reflective surfaces or even assisting to pick up dust.

Brushes

Make-up brushes, cotton buds, paintbrushes or even Pecs Pads are extremely useful for dusting and cleaning objects without disturbing your set, especially if you are photographing food.

Anti-Static Spray

Dust is a real problem, and it is not until you get your shoots to the post processing stage that you realize just how much dust is flying about. It can then take ages for you to heal and clone the specs of dust. However, an anti-static spray can remove the static from the item you are photographing and greatly reduce the amount of dust clinging to it.

Grips, Clips and Pins

Large and small, they are always useful. Bulldog clips are particularly good at gripping things such as paper, wire, mirrors and small reflectors, and they are available in a variety of different sizes. Grips on the other hand will enable you to quickly fasten two items together, such as wire and a stand.

If you are photographing clothes, then safety pins and butterfly clips will assist in shaping the clothing and holding the fabric.

Wire and Cable

Strong and stiff wire and cable can help you accurately place items in the frame, whilst minimizing intrusion. They can be quickly edited out in post processing.

Blu-Tack, Sticky Dots

Blu-Tack or some similar putty/non-permanent adhesive is perfect for holding small items in position, without blocking out the item. It is ideal when used with wire, cable and clips, plus it can help stabilize objects.

Tweezers

If you have large hands or are shooting small items, then a decent pair of tweezers will help you man oeuvre props and products and fine-tune your set with minimal disturbance.

Matting Spray

This spray is ideal if you are photographing very reflective and shiny products. The spray effectively removes the shine.

Water Atomizer/Spray

Water produced as a fine mist using a spray can be used to replicate condensation or add water droplets. Spray is most commonly used for drinks and plants. Remember: it is essential to exercise extreme care and caution when working with water close to electronic items, and especially hot lights.

Glass

If you are planning on photographing items such as drinks, then there are a variety of glass props you can buy, such as glass cubes and glass pellets to replicate ice cubes and crushed ice. These are even more convincing when used in conjunction with sprayed water.

Gloves

Lint-free cotton gloves and Pecs Pads are very useful when handling shiny and reflective items, such as steel and glass, to reduce the risk of fingerprints and dust.

Cleaning Products

During a shoot it is inevitable that something will get dirty and need cleaning. Try to stock up on a range of different cleaners and polishes to allow you to clean items without leaving marks.

Black Fabric

If you are shooting within a confined location or cluttered studio, you may find that you get unwanted reflections in your shots. A good work around is to suspend large pieces of black fabric to block off these reflections. Simply clamping the fabric to unused lighting stands can help you flag a large area very quickly.

Vinyl/Polycarbonate Board

Reflective vinyl board is extremely useful for placing items on, creating a mirror-like shadow or reflection. Depending on the thickness of the board, it can be ridged or flexible, so can also be curved and utilized as a background. Solid colors work best, as clear boards create a double reflection.

As it is so reflective, it usually requires less light to lift backgrounds and shadows, and more restraint may be needed to retain highlights, especially when using hard light sources.

Cameras and Lenses

You can use any type of camera or lens you wish to shoot still life, but some cameras and lenses work better than others. Traditionally, large format bellows cameras have been used for still life and products, which allow the lens to be tilted, thus correcting the issues associated with parallax errors. These cameras are specialty items and work on an entirely different format 35mm, plus usually require a digital or film back, further increasing the expense.

It is of course possible to utilize a longer focal length lens on your DSLR. Increasing your focal length to around 120mm and above will ensure that you fit the product you are shooting neatly into the frame, and exclude the unwanted studio interior, whilst minimizing distortion. However, using a standard lens is not suitable for every product and you may be required to correct perspective errors in Photoshop, which will dramatically increase your post processing time and begin to introduce unwanted artifacts into the photograph.

A little post processing is not an issue if you are only planning on shooting a few still life shoots, but if you are thinking about shooting still life and products commercially, then it is definitely worth investing in a few pieces of equipment. This does not mean that you have to sell your 35mm DSLR as there are affordable ways in which to quickly transform your DSLR into a highly flexible tilt and shift system that accepts large format lenses, giving you the best of both worlds. If you wish to use your 35mm or medium format based system, you may find that many manufacturers produce a tilt and shift lens. These lenses are traditionally more expensive than standard prime lenses, but will help correct some parallax issues.

Light Tent/Light box

A light tent is basically a pop-up box covered in a semi translucent or nylon white fabric. Specifications vary from manufacturer to manufacturer; however, you will generally find that the light tent has a removable panel, slit or hole in at least one side of the box, allowing the camera's lens to be pushed through. The white fabric is used to diffuse the light, in a similar way to a soft box, resulting in soft light whilst reducing unwanted reflections from immediate surroundings. Once erected, a product is positioned within the light tent and then it is lit externally by one or more studio lights.

This will to some degree produced a white surround in the finished photograph, allowing the object to be isolated and later cut out if necessary. The larger the light tent, the more lights will be required to obtain a pure high key background.

Light tents are a cost effective and space-saving alternative to a product table, as they are highly portable and very cheap. They are ideal for shooting smaller items and are generally used for e-commerce product photography.

Product Table/Tabletop Studio

Product tables (also known as tabletop studios) are available in several sizes and consist of a semi translucent piece of Perspex mounted onto a frame, which curves up at the rear of the table to form a seamless background. Products can be placed directly onto the Perspex or otherwise a paper background of your choice can be used and clamped onto the Perspex. The use of Perspex allows you to light products from underneath, whilst some of the larger and more expensive product tables will allow 4ft paper rolls to be mounted and the angle of the background to be raised and lowered. If you are shooting a lot of still life, then a quality table will be a worthwhile investment, offering considerably more flexibility than a light tent.

CHAPTER 4

HOW TO WELL-SHAPE THE FACE DURING PRODUCT PHOTOGRAPHY

Basic skills

Shaping the face is one of those important things that many photographers (whether amateur or professional) frequently neglect, yet it can instantly transform a photograph from an average shot into a good one. Everything revolves around the positioning of the face in relation to the light. Slight movement of the key light or the face is all that is required to shape the face. Controlling the light and the shadows in this way remains one of the underlying principles all studio-based photography.

In terms of photographing people, the four most commonly known principles are Short Lighting, Rembrandt Lighting, Broad Lighting and Butterfly Lighting. Other lighting styles that can be derived from these setups are Loop Lighting and Split Lighting. Understanding the basics re quires a little practice, but will help you achieve the best possible results every time.

Short Lighting

Short lighting lights the shortest side of the face, which is further from the camera (normally from cheek to cheek). Short lighting makes the face look slimmer and frequently brings out the shape of the mouth and cheeks. Quite often short lighting is the most flattering, especially when photographing people with rounder faces.

However, short lighting techniques are not always suitable for all subjects. For example, if your subject has a tall or long face, you may find that short lighting will make them look too thin. It also requires your subject to remain fairly static, because small movements of the head will change the lighting dramatically as the face moves in and out of the shadows.

HOW IT'S DONE

Sit your subject in front of the camera, positioning at a slight angle, so that the ear is facing the camera and the far eye is still visible.

Now move your key light so that it is approximately 90 degrees to the camera and raise it between 50cm and one meter higher than the subject, so that the catch light still remains in the eye. The height you position it will depend largely on the face of the subject and the size of the modifier you are using. The idea is to cast the shadows downwards, so that they shape the chin and the nose.

To fine-tune the lighting ask your subject to pose, then move the light around so that it lights the nearside cheek (cheek nearest the camera).

You will find that if your subject subsequently turns to face the camera completely, most of the front of the face will now be in the shadows, and only the ear and cheek will remain lit.

Short Rembrandt Lighting (including Split Lighting)

Rembrandt lighting takes its name from the paintings of Rembrandt, in which he used to paint a small inverted triangle of light under-eye on the shaded side of the face. This is caused by the light passing diagonally across the face, over the top of the nose and onto the cheek, creating the inverted triangle shape. In the first image, the Rembrandt lighting is derived from a short lighting technique. When used in this way it is particularly flattering to rounder faces.

However, it requires more control than standard short lighting as the small movements of the face towards the light will quickly result in a standard short lighting pattern, whilst movements away from the light will result in a split lighting effect.

Split lighting, on the other hand, is a little more dramatic and merely involves moving the light directly to the side of the subject, to light one side of the face only. This is sometimes achievable by getting the subject to directly face the camera within a short lighting setup. Its applications are somewhat limited, but it can be used to good effect on dark backgrounds, making the face disappear gradually into the shadows on the far side.

HOW IT'S DONE

To achieve the short Rembrandt lighting effect, sit your subject in front of the camera, positioning them at a slight angle, so that the ear is facing the camera and the far eye is still visible.

Now move your key light so that it is approximately 90 degrees to the camera and raise it between 50cm and 1 meter higher than the subject. The idea is that the catch light is at the 10 or 11 o'clock position in the eye if the light is positioned to camera left (or the one or two o'clock position if the light is positioned to camera right).

This will naturally throw the light downwards and across the face. The nose should shadow the cheek, whereas the light travelling over the bridge of the nose will light the area just under the eye.

It is of course possible to retain this effect even if your subject is facing directly towards the camera, and it requires you only to move the light when your subject changes position.

Broad Lighting (including Rembrandt Lighting)

Broad lighting is by far the most common form of lighting. It lights the broadest side of the face nearest the camera, that is, from ear to chin. Broad lighting setups are very flexible, in that they allow a subject to move more freely in front of the camera without the face being lost in the shadows. However, it is not always the most flattering of lighting and has a tendency to make people with rounder faces look much larger as it lights a greater area of the face. On the flip side, it is good for individuals that have tall or thin faces, which is why it is frequently used with professional models. You will also find it utilized in family portraits, especially with boisterous children that are difficult or impossible to keep still long enough to make use of any form of short lighting. Changes in position of the subject will easily change the broad lighting into a broad, head-on Rembrandt lighting pattern, also known as 'loop lighting'.

HOW IT'S DONE

Broad lighting is by far the most common approach to portrait photography.

Begin by positioning the studio light approximately 45 degrees off-axis to the camera and meter to approximately ƒ11. To shape the face with more shadows, simply move the light left or right around the camera axis. The further around to the side you move the light, the further into the shadow the far side of the face will be.

It is a good idea to start with the subject facing head-on to the camera and adjusting the light until the catch light is at the 10 or 11 o'clock position in the eye if the light is positioned to camera left (or the 1 or 2 o'clock position if the light is positioned to camera right). You will find that by doing this, the light will be flattering whether the subject is broad lit facing side-on or head-on.

By keeping the light in the same position and moving the subject, we can instantly change the shape of the face. As the subject moves and faces directly towards the camera, the shape of the face changes and the broad lighting can instantly become loop lighting, where the nose creates a looped shadow on the far side of the face.

By moving the light just a little further around the side of the subject, you can achieve a face-on Rembrandt lighting effect. The key to this remains the height and position of the key light.

Butterfly Lighting

Butterfly lighting refers to the shape of the shadow that is created under the nose. It is known for producing very dramatic lighting and is frequently used in fashion photography.

It is perhaps controlling the length of shadows that will make the greatest difference to this type of lighting. You will find that as the subject moves either left or right, the butterfly lighting actually becomes a broad lighting technique, so it is more suitable to subjects with a taller and slimmer face.

Lighting takes practice, but it should be fully understood if you are to build a solid foundation for your photographic career. It is also important to work quickly and professionally so that your subject doesn't lose interest and your shoot doesn't lose its impetus.

HOW IT'S DONE

In an ideal world, using a boom arm/stand makes your life a lot easier as it allows you to place the light closer to the subject without the stand blocking the field of vision between the camera and the subject. However, it is possible to use a regular lighting stand and place it directly behind you and the camera, although you will find that you have less flexibility over controlling the light and shadows as movement of the light stand is more restricted.

The light should be placed centrally to the subject if possible, so that it will cast the shadows downwards, resulting in more symmetrical lighting. Aim to get the catch light just under the eyelid or on the top of the cornea. You will find that the higher and closer the light source, the longer the shadows will be and the greater the risk of losing the catch light in the eye.

ONE HEAD LIGHTING TECHNIQUES

To illustrate the effects of shaping with light, let's use a single head fitted with a soft box, so that the light on the face may be clearly seen. It pays dividends to practice these techniques so that you are familiar with them when you are working on a commissioned shoot. You will find that friends and family will make willing subjects, and to prove that point, we will use a very fidgety five-year-old! It is one of those occasions where you have to work very quickly if you are to maximize the relatively short attention span of a young child. To help you visualize the light, also let's include a posterized image, clearly illustrating the highlights and shadows.

Using a single head can at times prove to be quite liberating for studio photographers, in as much as it affords them the ability to work simply, quickly and concentrate on the subject as opposed to the lighting. Relatively new photographers can be forgiven for thinking that working simply in this way undermines the technical prowess associated with studio lighting, yet it can achieve some stunning results.

It is the shape of the light and what you do with it that is important, and there are many different shapers and modifiers available to help you achieve different effects, from snoots to soft boxes. Hard light sources will help bring out sharp angles and increase the depth of shadows, whereas softer light sources will produce a more naturally flattering image. It is all about experimentation. Using a single light can help you concentrate on what is really important; drawing out the shapes and contours of your subject from all available angles.

The light and shadows are two contrasting opposites, which become more apparent when using a single light source. It is down to the photographer to control these elements and consider the overall tonality of the photograph.

Dark photographs with too many contrasting highlights can detract from subtle tones, whereas overly bright and specular photographs can lack both depth and tonality. With the help of some of the most basic pieces of equipment, such as the studio polyboard or bounce reflector, the photographer can help control the depth of the shadows and reduce the overall dynamic range of the photograph.

TWO HEAD LIGHTING TECHNIQUES

With two studio heads, photographers can be much more creative and have greater control over the light. The most frequent use of a second studio light is that of a 'fill light', which is used to control the depth of the shadows, whereas the main light or the 'key light' is used as the main light source and to add shape. The fill light is more cumbersome than the bounce reflector, but allows the photographer much greater control of how much shadow detail they desire. The caveat is that with greater control comes the necessity for more discipline and understanding of light and how it is used, plus the effects of the various modifiers and reflectors that are available.

There are of course many other creative ways in which to use a second light, either as a hair light, background light or even rims light. It's where you place and use it that makes all the difference.

THREE HEAD LIGHTING TECHNIQUES

Expanding from two heads to three heads will add a huge amount of flexibility to your setup. It is probably at this point that most photographers begin to fully develop their lighting skills, as the third light can be used to add several effects to both the subject and the backgrounds, without compromising on the use of a fill light when required. Understanding how to use this light effectively takes a little practice and requires more control and forethought. But with experimentation you will soon get to grips with some of the great techniques and effects you can achieve, eventually carving out your own style.

One common mistake made by many is not investing in additional reflectors and modifiers to use on an additional head, finding themselves limited as to how they can use it. It is important to invest in the right reflectors at the same time to help you adequately control and shape the light so your creativity is not hindered. So before you add a third light to your kit bag, factor in the price of some additional reflectors to keep your skills growing and your portfolio fresh.

FOUR AND FIVE HEAD LIGHTING TECHNIQUES

As you increase the number of lights you allow for more flexibility, but it can also mean more work and the need for additional control. However, it is of course possible to use all of the techniques that we have applied with the one, two and three head setups in a single shot, making the most of the shape, tone and texture of any subject.

One of the key principles of studio photography is to understand when to use more light. Quite often, inexperienced photographers will throw as much light as possible at a subject, without any cognizance of why they are lighting the subject and the particular aspects of the subject they need to draw out of the photograph. Remember that 'less is often more'.

Before you progress, think about the various aspects of additional lighting, such as side lighting, rim lighting, hair lights, gels and fill lighting. Which of these techniques will your subject and photograph benefit from? Try and picture the finished result and discard any lights and techniques that are not suitable.

CHAPTER 5

EXPLANATION TO BASIC RAW PROCESSING

T he word processing has been associated with photography since its existence. For many years it referred primarily to the processing of exposed film into negatives, which was done in temperature controlled tanks filled with chemicals to process the film and water to clean it. Once the negative was produced, the photographer used to process the photo graphs by placing the negatives onto an enlarger, thus exposing light sensitive paper to the light passing through the negative. The paper was then developed to produce the image, using developer, stop-bath and then a fixer. This was known as print processing. Generally speaking, once the film became a negative the ability to 'edit and retouch' began, with various darkroom techniques such as dodge and burn, although the choice of film and chemicals used to process the film could hugely affect the finished image.

Things have not changed much in the digital age, except that we now work with digital negatives or RAW files. To some degree the task of post processing images has become hugely more accessible and affordable, if not completely automated on some occasions. As most photographers no longer process film, the term post-processing has generally become accepted as anything that manipulates or changes the RAW file once the shutter has been fired.

Professional and experienced photographers tend not to rely on post processing techniques to save an image that does not succeed; however, some post processing is inevitable and to some degree expected in today's market.

Whilst I will cover a few RAW processing basics, it is important to bear in mind that the world of post processing, editing and editing software, such as Adobe Photoshop, are worth an entire book of their own. To this end, this chapter is a very brief and basic insight into how to process your RAW files using the industry standard software, Adobe Camera RAW (ACR).

RAW – THE DIGITAL NEGATIVE

Many people new to the world of digital photography fail to appreciate that their standard compact camera processes photographs in-camera. Any camera that shoots in JPEG or even TIFF format will process the images to some degree and then compress them into one of the recognized file formats.

JPEG may be convenient, allowing you to get many exposures on a single storage card; however, it also massively impacts on flexibility and image quality, introducing unwanted artifacts, color casts and tonal curves. RAW on the other hand undergoes no or little in-camera processing and needs importing into the camera manufacturer's proprietary software or a recognized RAW converter, such as Adobe Camera Raw, to be processed.

Shooting in RAW allows the photographer to process the images by way of fine-tuning and other adjustments prior to editing. The amount of adjustment that can be made to a digital negative prior to editing is huge, ranging from exposure to vignetting, so it is worth spending a little time exploring the various RAW processors on the market and the effects that you can achieve with them.

OTHER RAW CAPTURE UTILITIES

Note: For simplicity, I am referencing Adobe Camera RAW, as it is the most popular and widely available of RAW capture utilities. However, most major camera manufacturers, plus several third-party software developers, produce their own software to process RAW files. The techniques utilized here may be applied in the majority of RAW capture software; however, the tools and menus will vary.

There are a few useful basic tools and visuals you should be aware of when editing digital negatives that are particularly helpful when fine-tuning color balance, exposure and even reducing digital noise. These techniques are quick, basic and simple adjustments that will have you improving your images in minutes.

Histogram

The histogram will give you an instant visual graph of all the tonal information in your image. It will instantly tell you if you have clipped shadow detail or highlight detail. It will also give you a visual indication as to where the majority of the image data resides, such as the shadows, mid-tones or high-lights. The histogram is something that many new photographers ignore; however, it can be a very useful tool when judging exposure or even to ascertain if you are clipping certain colors.

When looking at the histogram, you will see shadow detail to the left, mid-tones in the middle and highlights to the right. As a rule of thumb, if your histogram is more dominant to the right, then your image is possibly overexposed.

On the other hand, if your histogram is more dominant to the left, then it is possible that your image is underexposed.

It is important to remember that it is only a guide and you will find that shooting on dark and light backgrounds may push the histogram either way, yet your photograph will be properly exposed.

If you are seeing a large spike in the histogram it is usually a sign of clipping (where image data is being lost). It may be that the dynamic range of the scene is wider than your camera can capture; however, small adjustments to exposure will usually help.

TEMPERATURE VS TINT

Remember: Adjusting the Temperature slider will make the photograph warmer or cooler, whereas the Tint slider compensates for the green or magenta tint.

Exposure Slider

It is always preferable to use a light meter and expose your images properly at the time of shooting. No amount of processing can beat a properly exposed photograph. However, there are of course times when exposure may not be as accurate as we had hoped for. It is common, even in studio photography and can be affected by subjects moving in and out of the light source or even by variances in power from cheaper flash heads. As you would expect, there are a few processing tweaks we can do when working with RAW files, but like everything, there is a caveat.

The Exposure slider essentially elongates the histogram and increases the clipping point of the highlights. Moving the slider to the right will lighten the image and moving it to the left will darken the image. The Exposure slider basically ascertains where the highlight data will clip, and then converts the clipped highlight value to 255. The remaining darker tones are lightened, and the histogram elongated and smoothed out.

All of this flexibility with exposure sounds great, but it is limited and its flexibility will depend entirely on the camera system you are using and the quality and bit depth of the image it produces. For the most part, increases above +1.00 can begin to introduce noise and artifacts into your photograph. You may also find that it causes shadow detail to break up and become posterized. The higher the ISO used, the more noticeable these artifacts can become. Higher-end 35mm systems and medium-format digital can be pushed further without necessarily experiencing any degradation of image quality.

Recovery Slider

Traditionally, it is the highlight information in digital photography that is the most susceptible to being blown. This is in contrast to film, where there is less latitude within the shadows. The studio, for the most part, is a controlled environment, where lighting can be adjusted to ensure that photographers achieve a properly exposed photograph without blowing the highlights; yet there are occasions when highlights are clipped, due to reflective surfaces, lighting and positioning constraints or even movement. The Recovery slider can help you retrieve some or all of the lost highlight data, and this is one of the huge benefits of shooting RAW.

You will find that moving the Recovery slider to the right will begin to slowly recover the highlights and as you move it, you will notice the highlight information on the histogram moving to the left and slowly bunching with the mid-tones. It is important to keep a close eye on the rest of the image, as pushing the slider too far will slowly begin to affect all of the lighter tones and can on some occasions make some highlights appear grey. Using the Recovery slider in conjunction with the Exposure slider will increase the rate of highlight recovery and retrieve most highlight data without the introduction of artifacts. It is an extremely useful and capable facility and it is possible to retrieve up to two f stops of information, but don't expect it to perform miracles!

Fill Slider

The Fill slider behaves like an artificial fill light. As you move the slider to the right you will see from the histogram how it will lift the shadow and mid-tone detail in the image, whilst the highlight detail remains stationary. It is particularly useful when you want to lift a small amount of shadow detail.

Moving the slider too far to the right will begin to produce some unusual effects and will begin to make a photograph looks as if it is solarized. Despite being a useful tool, it is no replacement for a properly positioned and metered fill light and is best when used sparingly.

Blacks Slider

True to its name, this slider adjusts the darkest or blackest parts of the image, by setting a new clipping point for the shadows. It is a useful tool for tackling slight overexposure or mild haze as it elongates the histogram, pulling it down to the left whilst leaving the highlights intact and increasing the contrast within the shadows. The Blacks slider can be used to complement adjustments with the Fill slider if the image begins to look a little flat and lifeless.

It is worth remembering, though, that you are basically clipping the shadow detail out of the image before you export it into your editing software, so it is worth considering what further post-processing will be done and whether you could utilize some of that shadow detail later on.

Brightness Slider

Brightness should not be confused with the Exposure slider as they perform different tasks. Whereas the Exposure slider concentrates on the highlights, pushing the histogram to the right, the Brightness slider tends to concentrate on expanding the mid-tones whilst compressing the highlights. As you adjust the Brightness slider, the mid-tones push to the right, lightening the image.

Many photographers neglect the Brightness tool in favor of adding a tone curve during post processing. Yet it remains very useful when used in conjunction with the Blacks and Exposure slider as a way of making those final adjustments to the equally important mid-tones. Like any adjustment, it needs to be done in moderation as too much can begin to make an image appear washed out and lacking in contrast.

Contrast Slider

Every photograph needs contrast; otherwise it would look flat and lifeless. The task is to strike the right balance between the shadows and highlights, whilst keeping enough detail in the mid-tones. The Contrast slider is one of the tools I rarely use as there are many other more precise ways to add contrast. Even when processing RAW files, it is possible to increase contrast using a combination of the Blacks and Exposure sliders, before editing a parametric or point based tone curve. The Contrast slider basically elongates the histogram, stretching the mid-tones whilst compressing both the shadows and the highlights. It reality, it is the layperson's way of adding contrast and is best left for those quick fixes or batch processing contact sheets.

Clarity, Vibrance and Saturation

These three sliders are located under the Contrast slider in Adobe Camera Raw, and they are for the professional studio photographer, as more precise adjustments can be made later on during post processing.

1) Clarity

The Clarity slider increases or decreases the contrast around the edges, which gives the impression that the image looks sharper. If you are processing high contrast black and white street photography or environmental portraits with lots of texture, then the Clarity slider when pushed to the right may prove to be very useful. If you are working with models or even family portraits, however, then it is definitely one to avoid, as it has a tendency to pick out every imperfection – definitely not what most people want, and it will double the amount of healing and cloning during post processing.

2) Vibrance

The Vibrance slider makes the image look more vibrant by way of increasing the saturation of the colors without clipping the already well saturated areas. When pushed too far, it can make an image look rather false, as all the colors look too even, so less is definitely more. For studio work the use of the Vibrance control is limited, unless you are batch processing contact sheets, as more precise adjustments can be made during the later stages of post processing.

3) Saturation

When increased, the Saturation slider increases the color throughout an image, causing the colors that were already strong to be clipped. It can of course also decrease the color, but tends to produce a rather flat and uninteresting black and white image. Unless you are batch processing, the Saturation slider is better left untouched, and instead an adjustment layer made in the latter stages of post processing.

DETAIL TAB

By moving along the tabs located under the histogram, you will come across the Detail Tab. By selecting this tab, you open up the options to vary the sharpening and add an element of noise reduction if necessary. Both the Sharpening and Noise Reduction sliders are very useful tools, but care needs to be taken when using them as they can introduce unwanted artifacts into the image. It is important to remember that once the RAW image has been processed and exported into your editing software it has the ability to become more destructive the more you edit. Your use of the Sharpening and Noise Reduction sliders will of course depend entirely on your given market. So if you are photographing a hundred portraits a day and then batch processing the lot, the detail tab will be ideal for your workflow.

However, if you are shooting commercially and will be editing a small number of photographs, you may wish to leave much of the sharpening to the later stages of post production, where parts of the image can be masked and the layers peeled back if necessary or adjusted to the output size and medium.

SHARPENING

Amount

As it suggests, moving the slider adjusts the strength of the sharpening. Moving the slider to the right increases the sharpening and moving it to the left decreases it. It is worth watching the image as you increase the sharpening, as too much has a tendency to produce halos and pixilation around contrasting edges. Default value is 25.

Radius

This is the area around or within a pixel where the sharpening will take effect i.e. the width of the halos. Increasing the radius basically increases the area that is sharpened, or, adjusts the size of the details that sharpening is applied to.

Using a smaller radius will allow you to sharpen smaller and more subtle parts of the image, whereas a larger radius may assist you in correcting minor motion blur. A larger radius setting will also emphasize the finer edges and at the same time enhance the softer edges. Default value is 1.0.

Detail

The Detail slider suppresses the halo effects whilst allowing you to increase the Amount of sharpening without unwanted artifacts. When the Amount and Radius sliders are at their default values, the effect of the Detail slider is fairly subtle and is useful for bringing the fine edges of hair and fabric, even when pushed to the maximum value of 100. However, multiply this with a sharp increase with the Amount slider and the effect is immediate and unpleasant, producing unwanted noise and artifacts. For studio portraits, lower detail settings are recommended.

Masking

The Masking slider affords you some control over the overall sharpening effect. The more you increase the Masking slider, the more you begin to protect the flatter tones within the image from the effects of the sharpening. Utilizing the grayscale edge mask by holding down the key will help you visualize your adjustments more clearly.

NOISE REDUCTION

Noise is caused by several factors within the camera. This can be anything from the heat generated by the sensor, in- camera processing or even exposure times.

Noise reduction (NR) is a very useful way of removing unwanted noise from images. As a rule, noise isn't a common issue with studio photography, given that most images will be taken between 100 and 200 ISO and be correctly exposed. However, there may be occasions when you find that you need to increase your ISO to compensate for depth of field or lack of power. It is occasions such as this when underexposure is a risk and where noise can begin to creep into the shadow areas. Applying noise reduction during RAW processing and post processing is for the most part better than doing it in- camera, simply because you have greater control over the whole process and will avoid introducing unwanted artifacts at the early stages. Noise reduction is destructive and if applied during RAW processing it becomes permanent. For this reason, it is advisable to leave noise reduction until the later stages of editing, so that it may be applied selectively and peeled back when necessary.

LUMINANCE

The Luminance slider controls the type of noise we most commonly known as grain, also known as grayscale noise.

The default value in ACR is '0', so moving the slider to the right will increase the noise reduction and decrease the film grain. It is important not to increase this too much as it will begin to remove the detail. Grain is rarely an issue, adds character to an image and is even less noticeable when printing.

Luminance Detail and Luminance Contrast

Unless you are shooting at very high ISO or pushing the exposure on a much underexposed image you are unlikely to benefit too much from using these sliders.

The Luminance Detail slider controls the luminance noise threshold. On the face of it, the higher the value the more detail and noise it will return to the image, although the detail is more apparent on the edges, leaving the flatter tones looking smooth.

The Luminance Contrast slider is useful for very noisy images. When used at higher values, it will assist in preserving the contrast, but will also introduce blotches of noise and mottling.

COLOR

The Color slider default is set at 25. It is not unusual in studio photography for the default setting to be zeroed in order to preserve the original color. If you have noise in your image, moving this slider to the right will begin to remove the colored speckles that you can see in noisy images, which are normally red, purple and green, known as chroma. Increase the Color noise reduction too much and the image will become blotchy.

Color Detail

The Color Detail slider controls the color noise threshold. It is there to assist in reclaiming some of the detail removed by Color noise reduction. Pushing the slider to the right will protect finer, detailed color edges, but increase color speckling. Decreasing the amount of Color Detail will remove colored speckles at the risk of introducing color bleed.

LENS CORRECTIONS TAB

The Lens Corrections tab offers a range of lens profiles to fit a range of common lenses from different lens manufacturers. The lens corrections compensate for the three most common lens aberrations, namely vignetting, geometric distortion and lateral chromatic aberration. By selecting the lens manufacturer and the lens used to take the photograph, ACR will then make a series of adjustments based on the lens calibration data available.

Correction Amount

Once your chosen lens has been selected, the three grayed out adjustment sliders under the Correction Amount heading will become available.

Distortion and Chromatic Aberration

The Distortion slider will allow you to fine-tune bends in parallel and horizontal edges/lines, such as barrel or pincushion distortion. The Chromatic Aberration slider will help remove color fringing along high contrast edges. You will find that overuse of these sliders can frequently correct some areas of the photograph, whilst causing issues in others.

VIGNETTING

Vignetting is basically the gradual light fall-off that can be experienced towards the corners of a photograph. It is more prolific when using wide lenses, very long zooms and wide apertures. For studio work that is shot on standard lenses at apertures between $f8.0$ and $f16$ it is rarely a major issue. In fact it can actually prove to be fairly useful for portrait photographers as the gradual light fall-off assists in reducing the plainness of paper backgrounds, whilst making the viewer focus on the subject in the middle. Portrait and wedding photographers frequently add vignetting to their images.

Ultimately, how you use this RAW process will depend entirely on your workflow and intended results. It may be easier to remove a vignette globally than to add one. It should be applied in the same way as many other corrections and effects prior to post processing. If it is possible to leave it until later on in post processing, then this would afford you more flexibility over the finished image. On the other hand, if you are batch-processing hundreds of images, it may be worth applying it globally to many images at the same time.

There are two common types of vignetting:

PHYSICAL VIGNETTING

This is usually apparent in the extreme corners of the lens and usually caused by a physical object intruding on the lens, such as a lens hood or lens filters. This will usually require cloning or cropping.

INTERNAL VIGNETTING

This is most often caused by the optical elements inside the lens and is easily correctable using software or by stopping down. If you are using a full-frame DSLR then you may suffer from the effects of vignetting more often than with a system utilizing a cropped sensor.

EFFECTS TAB

Post-Crop Vignetting As opposed to a lens correction, the Post-Crop Vignetting tool under the Effects tab is intended to be used artistically, rather than as a lens correction.

Style

The Style has a drop down menu offering you three choices: Highlight Priority, Color Priority and Paint Overlay.

Highlight Priority- will apply a vignette whilst protecting the contrast within the highlights, but may cause color shifts within the shadow areas.

Color Priority- preserves color hues but can reduce the detail within the highlights.

Paint Overlay- will blend the colors within the image with a black or white vignette, with a possibility of reducing the contrast within the highlights.

Amount

Moving the slider to the right will lighten the corners of the image, whereas moving the slider to the left will darken them.

Midpoint

An increase in the Midpoint slider will restrict the area of adjustment near the corners, whereas a decrease will apply the adjustment to a larger area from the corners.

Roundness

Increasing the values by pushing the slider to the right will make the effect more circular, where moving the slider to the left will begin to make the effect more oval.

Feather

Higher values will begin to increase the feathering between effect and the surround pixels. Reducing the values will perform the opposite.

Highlights (Highlight Priority and Color Priority)

This controls the punchiness of the highlights, such as the glow from various continuous light sources.

CHAPTER 6

STILL LIFE PHOTOGRAPHY

There is a popular misconception that shooting products is a simple job, whereas it is in fact the complete opposite. Having done a lot of research concerning product photography, becoming a real expert in this field requires a lot of commitment and for those who are professional their experience shows there is an immense amount of time and skill that goes into setting up each shot.

A lot, of course, depends on the end use of each shot, so products placed onto a white background for e-commerce take less technical knowledge and time than those produced for major manufacturers and luxury brands. However, each shot still needs time and consideration, even for mass marketing and retail, and spending time getting the lighting and angles right will save you hours of tedious post processing work later on. The less time spent behind the computer, the better.

CONSIDERATIONS

Backgrounds

It sounds like common sense, but the background scenery behind the product can be as important as the product itself.

In the same way as commercial fashion and beauty, products sell a lifestyle and usually have a brand identity. The props and background help set the scene generate the identity and place it within the right market, but at the end of the day it is meeting the expectations of the consumer that really counts.

E-commerce

Photographs on the internet allow the long distance consumer to see what they are buying. E-commerce is essentially the nitty-gritty of still life photography and the photographs need to be clean, bright and without distractions.

This calls for a simple background, and by far the most popular choice for this is white, followed by grey and black.

Using a plain background allows designers to easily cut out the product and use it elsewhere. It is of course always possible to use other colors – after all there are no rules. However, this choice will ultimately depend on the finish and color of the product, or even the design of the website or catalogue. It is important to remember that brighter colors are more distracting, and they can occasionally result in color casts, so they tend to be used less frequently for ecommerce and catalogue shots.

Lifestyle

Every product has a target audience and this audience will have a particular lifestyle. Setting the scene for this by placing the product within a properly designed set can work wonders. Many sets found in the glossy magazines have had large budgets and props specifically bought in; however, lifestyle can also be showcased by simply propping the product with a few carefully placed items. If you search around, you can find a range of items to prop your products, such as flowers, pebbles and even liquids. As for backgrounds, a little imagination can be equally as creative, with photographers using everything from fabrics or wallpaper to raw materials such as concrete and steel in their backgrounds.

Static or Dynamic

Part of placing the product and creating the lifestyle is how the product itself is portrayed. Movement or a sense of movement within a product shot can make the scene more dynamic and energetic, whereas static sets will look more classic and subdued. Your choice as to whether you make the set more dynamic or static should really depend on the product you are shooting and the intended audience. For example an invigorating facial wash will work well with a sense of movement, especially water with bright colors.

Cold drinks and beers are enhanced by ice and condensation. Classic jewellery on the other hand works better within a more static and often subdued set, so that the viewer can concentrate on the beauty of the jewellery. So it is important to visualize the context–dropping a 24-carat gold and diamond studded ring into water may not appeal to the target market, while a static shot of a shampoo or shower gel may look rather uninspiring and lack-luster.

BASIC STILL LIFE TECHNIQUES

A large light tent is perfect for lighting smaller items; helping isolate the subject, create a clean white surround and reducing unwanted reflections. The beauty of the light tent is its simplicity. The light is diffused by the panels of the light tent and then bounces around inside the box, helping to lift both the background and the shadows. It is possible to use only a single light with a light tent; however, the results will vary depending on the size of the box, positioning of the light and the item being photographed.

The following example has been split into three, building up from using a single light, up to three lights, so you should see the subtle difference each head makes to the photograph.

There is no magic formula as to how many lights you should use when shooting with a light tent. A lot can depend on the shade of the background you are using and whether or not you require more or less shadow detail. For example, if you were to use a standard white paper background, you might find that the shadows remain quite dark. Most back ground papers have a matt finish and are therefore less reflective than a glossy vinyl. If you wish to lift the shadows, then you will need to use either a reflector or a second light.

Conversely, if you are using a reflective vinyl background that bounces light everywhere, you will find that the shadows are much lighter, possibly negating the need for a second light.

A lot can also depend on your workflow. It is of course preferable to get the shot as perfect as possible 'in camera', reducing the need for post processing. However, if you are only photographing a small number of items, it is perfectly acceptable to extract these from the background during post processing. If you are shooting hundreds of items, then relying on post processing is the last thing you want to do, as this will dramatically increase your workload and reduce your profit margin. The moral is, don't resort to post processing unless you really have to. Instead, add additional lights as and when they are needed and light the photograph properly.

CHAPTER 7

DIGITAL PHOTOGRAPHING COMES WITH NUMEROUS MERITS

Instant review

If there's one thing that's made digital photography more popular than film ever was it's the ability to review the picture just taken. How can you ever learn if you have to wait for pictures to come back from a lab and the experience of the time has long since faded. With digital you can review your picture, learn from what has or hasn't worked and reshoot if necessary. Don't trust the brightness of the LCD picture though. They are designed to show all images with normal brightness. To really see whether it's a good exposure use the ability to check the Histogram of the image. This should show tones and data across the spread of the image.

If there are gaps at the black end or the white end it means the picture is overexposed or underexposed. If white elements have no detail at all it means that the exposure has blown highlights. Underexposed photos can be rescued to a degree with photo editing. Blown highlights are lost data, requiring skilful work to replace and in many cases it simply won't be possible. It's harder to see if a picture is in sharp focus because everything on 2" LCD looks sharp. If you suspect that the conditions were tricky and the result might be out of focus, take two shots, or use the zoom into the image on playback to check.

Erasable pictures

If a photo is duff because the lighting is wrong, the subject moved, the composition looks poor, etc, then the digital advantage is that after review you can delete and shoot again.

It also gives you the power to sneak in that extra shot at the end of the day. Say your memory cards are full but you have just spotted a beautiful sunset at a photogenic location free of tourists. Your film-using Neanderthal buddy will be cursing his bad luck since he's used all his stock, but you get the photo because you can insert any of your memory cards at any point, go through the pictures you've got and make that decision to delete one to make room for the prize winning shot.

There is another digital advantage tied into this theme and that is one of resolution. Just because your camera can shoot 12Mp pictures it doesn't mean to say that you always want to, because, the bigger the picture size, the more room the photo files take up on the memory card.

For happy snaps of the family on holiday you can stick to lower resolutions that will be fine for 6x4 prints later, but give you considerably more shots to store on the cards you have. You aren't tied to using one resolution per memory card, you can shoot any size at any point and save those 12Mp pictures for that sunset we were just talking about. Later, when you have downloaded the pictures from the card you can use it again, over and over until you wear it out. In the case of sturdy Compact Flash cards this will take some doing.

Digital ISO

All film is rated at a certain ISO number which generally refers to how fast it can react to light. This is based on the size of the grain in the material; the bigger the grain, the faster it reacts. The reason for having different ISO rated film is obvious. If conditions are quite dark or gloomy, there is not enough light to enable the camera to be used with recourse to a tripod.

If you attempt to hand hold the camera in low light then the slow shutter speed will capture the wobble despite your best attempts to hold the camera steady and the resulting photo will be blurred. With a faster ISO film, it reacts more quickly to the light - the camera knows this and so can use a faster shutter speed, making it safe to hand hold.

There's a quick rule of thumb you can apply, when face with falling levels of light. If the shutter speed is less than the focal length of the lens, then camera shake becomes increasingly likely. For wide angle shots at say 28mm, it means that you can shoot at 1/28th of a second before really worrying about camera shake. But, if using a telephoto lens at say 300mm, then anything less than 1/300th of a second is going to problematic. This is only a rough guide because if you have rock steady hands you can shoot at lower speeds and if you have shaky hands, the problems arrive earlier.

For instance, some of you would never shoot at 28mm with anything less than 1/50th of a second. Back to that film stock then, the downside of higher ISO rated film is that with the grain being larger, the picture looks; coarser, Fine for moody jazz clubs or salty, monochrome fisherman photos, but not so good for fresh faced models and children. The other problem is that once the film is in the camera you can't change it until the film is all used up so if the sun comes out you either have to live with grainy photos or waste the rest of the film.

Enter the digital camera which also uses the same ISO rating system. How come though, since digital doesn't use film grain? When taking a photo the shutter is kept open for a set period of time, regardless of how fast it might be, it is not instant, and so for the duration of that time, light accumulates in the CCD/CMOS. When the exposure finishes the level of light in each diode is turned into a charge value that is sent to be processed. However, the analogue to digital conversion system only looks at a limited range of values - this is exactly like the exposure latitude in film. Digital is more like slide film than print film.

The reason for this is a technical one, based on how the light is captured and the speed of hardware processing. However, to get back on track, anything above this range of light values becomes white, anything below it, black. The range of exposure is carefully worked out in the factory before production begins and is optimized to produce as noise free an image as possible with shutter speed settings that relate to the quality and responsiveness set up by the ISO system parameters.

if the conditions are dark then the camera needs longer shutter speeds to let enough light in for a correct exposure. The longer the shutter speed, the more chance that any movement will be recorded as camera shake, as explained. The alternative is to change the ISO setting for the photo from the usually default 100, to 200. This tells the camera to perform the analogue to digital conversion in half the time that an ISO100 shot would need for a good quality, perfect exposure. When using the camera in a program mode like Aperture Priority it means that the camera can increase the shutter speed by double the amount. So, an ISO100 quality picture that, in gloomy conditions, needed a 1/8th of a second exposure, at ISO200 will use 1/16th of sec, unless you put it in manual mode. If you increase the ISO to 400 it double the shooting speed available again so now the camera will use 1/ 32th second, which may be fast enough to avoid camera shake.

There is a payoff for this, because you can't get faster speeds for nothing. There isn't any more light available, and you are taking the shot in less time, so you are forcing the camera to create an exposure with less than what it ideally - that ideal being ISO100 - needs. What you need to know is that the higher ISO ratings and long exposures both introduce digital noise which is due to fluctuations in recording the light because the shutter was not open long enough to get the quality of recording that ISO 100 dictates. The higher the ISO you use, whether it be 400, 800, 1600 the faster the shutter speed you can use, but the more digital noise there will be in the picture. Digital noise is not like grain from faster film, it is literally variations in the image that show up as pixels that are the wrong color. Digital noise is often green in shadow areas.

The digital advantage is that you can change the ISO rating for every single shot you take, so if you are on holiday and go inside an old building then you can switch to ISO 200, but when back outside again, switch back to ISO 100 in the sunlight. For even better quality, some cameras use lower ISO ratings like 50, for better tonal quality and color saturation.

Automatic White Balance

The next digital advantage is something usually surprises beginners who are introduced for the first time to the new era of digital photo shooting. It's called Automatic White Balance or AWB for short. Film cameras don't have it and struggle with the consequences. Digital cameras do. They also have manual white balance settings and some have configurable white balance settings as well.

The problem is that light gives off a color cast depending on the conditions. Light has a color temperature value measured in degrees Kelvin. It starts off low with reddish and orange colors down at around 2500K, it becomes white, at around the time of the midday sun, which is around 5600K and it gets blue when there is cloud cover over the sky, which can have a temperature up to 10,000K. Regular film is designed for use in average daylight conditions. The problem comes when it gets gloomy or worse still, you move indoors and go under tungsten and fluorescent lighting.

These two light types have considerably lower color temperatures than daylight and these results in yellow and an awful sickly green cast respectively. Either flash is needed, but if that isn't practical, color filters have to be used and these are hopelessly hit and miss. You can also get tungsten rated film and use that. However, this is obviously a messy situation, but the good news is that digital cameras can cope with this by processing the image to remove the cast. Whenever you focus and get a meter reading from your digital camera, if you are using Automatic White Balance, it also assesses the color temperature and switches accordingly. This ensures that you get pictures that are clean and white, rather than yellow and green.

Now, this happens automatically, hence AWB, but it isn't infallible. Many digital cameras have manual white balance settings in the menu. If you find that your indoor snaps in low light make the people in them look pink, then you need to manually select a color temperature from those on offer.

Don't worry, although the color temperature scale is expressed in thousands of degree Kelvin, most cameras simply offer settings using familiar icons for the lighting type you are shooting under. Select the right type and carry on snapping, but don't forget to reset it to normal when you go outdoors.

PASM and Program Mode

On the top dial of many cameras is that mysterious set of letters, P, A, S, M. On other cameras you may see P, Av, Tv and M. They mean exactly the same, but are less obvious. Only higher end compact cameras use these, and most will have them in a menu rather than on a dial. These are the functions you will see on all DSLRs. There are also other symbols as well, but these are the ones you need to use in order to take control of your photography.

What these letters stand for, are Program mode, Aperture Priority, Shutter Priority and Manual and are the four main ways of controlling how your camera takes a picture. When you press the fire button on a camera it activates the automatic focus which locks on to the object in the focus area. At the same time, a system inside the camera known as the metering, evaluates how much light is out there. The result, which is what is required to achieve a good exposure in which there are details throughout the dark and light areas of the scene, is known as the Exposure Value or EV. The camera then uses the two features it has under its control to produce an exposure that matches the EV. The two features it has are the aperture of the lens and the shutter speed of the lens.

The aperture is the hole in the lens that the light comes through and is used in much the same way that the iris in your eye works. When there is a lot of light your iris narrows to let less in, when it is dark it goes as wide as possible to let in as much as possible. The lens aperture works in exactly the same fashion except that it is controllable rather than automatic. A wide open aperture let's a lot of light in at once, a narrow aperture let's a small amount of light in at once.

The shutter speed is used to control how long the light is allowed to hit the CCD/CMOS because photography is all about volume of light rather than instants. When people say a photograph is an instant moment frozen in time, they're wrong. It isn't. It's a short period of time where the occupants were not moving much. Anyway, when the exposure period starts the shutter is closed; there are no values in the CCD/CMOS. The shutter opens for a set period and light floods in. When the exposure ends the shutter closes again and the light values are counted in the CCD/CMOS as explained earlier.

The upshot of this is that by using a combination of the aperture and shutter speed the camera produces the correct exposure for the scene it sees. This is in effect what the Program modes do. Its automatic modes for those times when you do not have time to set the shot up, you just need to shoot it. However, Program mode doesn't offer any creative control, because there are implications to the choice of aperture or shutter speed.

Aperture Priority

Here, you set the aperture value yourself and the camera sets the shutter speed to generate the correct exposure. Why would you want to do this? Simply, the depth of field, Depth of field is the amount of a scene that is in sharp focus from front to back. If you use a wide aperture then you get less depth of field, if you use a narrow aperture you get the most depth of field.

Apertures are expressed as f-stops with the standard range going f/2.8, f/4, f/5.6, f/8, f/11, f/16, f/22. As the range goes up, each f-stop lets in half as much light as the previous one but creates more depth of field. You can also get higher f-stops and lower ones, which are particularly useful for low light and portraits. On compact cameras the f- stop range is built in to the camera because the lens is built in, but on DSLRs, the f-stops are unique to each lens, so you can for example, buy a 50mm lens with an f/1.4 value, specifically for portraits with out of focus backgrounds. The most common uses for aperture control are to use wide apertures, which means a low f-stop number, on portraits so that the background becomes indistinct and does not interfere with the subject, putting full weight on the subject, and narrow apertures in landscape photography, which are high f-stop numbers, so that as much of the landscape is in sharp focus as possible.

What should be pointed out here is that because of the smaller lens and CCD sizes on compact cameras you get roughly 4-5 times more depth of field at an f-stop compared to a film camera. This means that f/2.8 is more like f/11-f/16, making it hard to get a background out of focus in a portrait shot. Digital SLRs which do not use full frame chips (that is a CCD or CMOS that is the same size as 35mm film), generally create depth of field associate with half an f-stop more than that being used.

However, back to compacts, it doesn't mean that when you use f/8 you are getting f/64 or better levels of depth of field the quality of the CCD and lens are much lower than SLRs so any high end advantage is lost, it simply helps control the exposure.

There are two other times when you might want to take control of the aperture. If it is quite dingy and there is little light you will want the aperture as wide open as possible to let in the maximum amount of light. Equally, if the day is very bright, you might want to use a narrower aperture to restrict the amount of light.

A final consideration for aperture settings is this. The sharpness of a lens is not consistent throughout and the sharpest part is when it uses an aperture of f/8 or f/11. If you don't need a great deal of depth of field because there's not much of interest in the background then use this setting to get the subject as sharp as possible.

Shutter Priority

This brings us on to Shutter Priority and it will come as no surprise to read that here you set the shutter speed and the camera works out the aperture value that will generate the correct exposure. Why would you want to control the shutter speed? Consider this: You are at a waterfall. If you set the camera to 1/250th of a second you will freeze every falling water droplet in the photo. If you set it to a two second exposure that frozen water will instead turn into a creamy blurred flow while the background remains perfectly sharp.

If you want to catch a horse jumping over a fence then a fast shutter speed will freeze it at the pivotal time, a slow shutter speed will show the horse as a blur over the fence. Aside from these creative considerations there are also practical ones. When light levels are falling the evaluated shutter speed will fall too and if it drops beneath 1/15th of a second then you run the risk of inadvertent camera shake (also, refer back to the comment on focal length previously). This is because you cannot hold the camera steady enough during the exposure and the slight movements all register in the final picture. At fast shutter speeds the exposure time is so short that it is all over before your hand has time to move slightly.

It is not magic though, if there isn't enough light the camera might not be able to set a wide enough aperture to give a good exposure. In this case the camera will warn you that the picture is going to be underexposed. The solution is to either increase the ISO rating or to use a slower shutter speed. The converse applies as well, and this is most likely to happen when trying to photograph waterfalls during bright daylight.

Here's why. A typical reading for daylight would be an aperture of f/8 and 1/125th sec shutter speed. So let's move these numbers around. This is the same amount of light as f/11 at 1/64th sec, then f/16 at 1/32nd sec, f/22 at 1/16th sec. At this point you have run out of available apertures on your wide angle lens and you're still way off getting the two second exposures to blur the water of that waterfall. You would actually need an aperture of f/128 which is the kind of narrowness you only get on a pinhole camera. So clearly, even if you do set the shutter speed to 2secs in SP mode the camera is not going to be able to give you the right aperture because there's just too much daylight.

The solution in this particular case is to use neutral density filters over the lens which reduce the amount of light coming into the camera. The point is though, that there's generally more flexibility using AP mode than SP mode, but both need the amount of light to be within certain parameters or you need to change the sensitivity of the camera or reduce the volume of light.

Manual Mode

The final picture mode is Manual and on this one, you set both the aperture and the shutter speed. Now this may seem very strange to a beginner because if you are to set both factors, how do you know what settings to use? There are two main uses for the manual setting: the first is when using an off-camera flash system, the second is when taking photos at night. In the first instance you cannot use the built in metering to help out because the flash hasn't gone off yet. Using built in flash is different because the camera controls the flash itself and switches it off when it thinks there is enough light in the picture. When using off-camera flash, or studio flash as it is usually called, all the camera does is activate it, it doesn't control it, More on flash shortly.

The other use of Manual is long exposures and these typically take place at night when shooting landscapes where you need decent depth of field. The reason why manual needs to be used is because the camera is designed to evaluate light within a certain range and once it falls below that level it can't really tell what it should be. Because of this AP and Program mode normally have a limit of around 8 seconds for the shutter speed. If you need it to be longer, you need to use manual mode.

So, it's after sunset, you set the camera to f/16 in AP mode and the shutter speed will be out of range, the camera can't work it out. Either a hand held specialist light meter is called for, or you can set the camera to the widest aperture that lets in the most light. This gives you a certain shutter speed reading. Then, a bit of math's is employed. Say, at f/2, you got a shutter speed of half a second. At f/2.8, you'd need 1 second, at f/4, 2 seconds, at f/5.6, 4 seconds, at f/8, 8 seconds, at f/11, 16 seconds, and finally, at say f/16, you'd need a 32 second exposure. You can only set that in manual. It should be pointed out again that many point and shoot compacts don't have either the control or the shutter speeds required for this, so we're really talking about DSLRs here.

For instance, here is an interesting example using Manual mode. The main camera exposure is set to record the background properly so that it is metered first. It gives results of 1/6th of a sec at f/5.6. On top of this, a manual flash-gun is also used and this is set to the same aperture of f/5.6. The speed of the flash is very fast, so it's only on for an instant but it puts out enough light to illuminate the subject.

The key point is that this type of flashgun power is measured in terms of aperture only, the speed is relatively unimportant because the flashgun delivers all the light, essentially at once. As the apertures matches and the camera shutter speed plus the aperture gives a perfect background, they combine together perfectly.

Metering & exposure compensation

All digital cameras have a metering system. A metering system is a set of firmware evaluation routines that kick in when you press the fire button to get focus lock. A further pressing of the fire button will take the picture. The object of metering is to create an exposure (aperture plus shutter speed) that is in the middle of the range of tones that it can see, which will then be translated, on the digital picture, into an image with black-white tones, centered on 18% grey, which is the mid-tone. This is a tricky concept to understand at times when dealing with very light or very dark pictures. There are three main types of metering system: zone, spot and centre weighted.

Zone metering- is a general purpose system that splits the scene it sees through the lens into small squares. Some cameras have 9 zones, others have 49. Either way, the camera assesses the light values in each of those zones, adds them together and comes up with an average. It then selects an exposure value that is going to cover the maximum number of the zone values it sees. This exposure value or EV is then used by the program modes in working out the exact aperture and shutter speed combination.

Usually, this metering system does a good job and the result is spot on however, there are times when it gets it wrong or places the wrong emphasis. A typical example is when there is a very bright sky which overloads the emphasis onto exposing for the sky, resulting in the ground coming out murky. Or when there is water involved because water is very reflective and will fool the sensors into thinking that the scene is brighter than it really is.

spot metering- this uses a circular area in the middle of the photo and assesses the light from there only. It ignores whatever else is going on the photo. This isn't the end of the story because the common misconception is that whatever you've taken a photo of and it's usually people - will be perfectly exposed. What happens is that whatever the spot focuses on, will be the mid-tone grey of the final picture. It's tricky to see this when you are looking at things in color, particularly as certain colors give the impression of being brighter or darker than they really are. Some examples here will make the concept clearer.

Take a white card and manually focus on it. Use spot metering to read the exposure and take the picture. What is the result, a white card in the photo? No, it's grey. 18% grey in fact.

Look at a histogram of the picture and all the data will be centered around the middle. Repeat the same experiment with a black card and the result is… exactly the same. Grey. Whenever you take a photo, all the metering systems are trying to give you an exposure based around this middle reading, which is why scenes with lots of black can be overexposed so they are muddy black and scenes with lots of white (like snow) are often underexposed so you get dirty White.

The real practical use of spot metering is when challenging circumstances are guaranteed to fool the zone metering system such as bright skies and you know this so use spot metering to look around the scene for what you think is going to be the mid-point of the exposure. Now it must be said, as was explained earlier, that there is a limit to the exposure latitude in digital cameras, and scenes with extreme lighting usually cannot be captured successfully. If you have a very bright sky you really should use filters to darken it down so that it falls within the parameters of what the camera can capture in one shot.

Centre-weighted metering- is a combination of the two previous modes. The greatest emphasis is placed on what is in the centre, but account is taken of the rest of the zones of the photo. It simply gives more emphasis to a central object.

This is certainly a useful mode for outdoor portrait shots since first and foremost your subject will be well exposed but not wholly at the expense of the background. In many regards, centre weighted is a very good metering system to use if there is something that commands more attention than the picture as a whole. The centre spot places the subject in the middle of the exposure, then the residual zone reading adjusts the exposure up or down according to the brightness or darkness of everything else.

Metering is a fine thing and usually does a good job, but there are times when it doesn't and checking the LCD will show if a photo is dramatically under or overexposed. Rather than trying the other metering modes – you have to know when and why to use them – there is a simple solution at hand. This is known as Exposure Compensation and is available on virtually all cameras.

On mainly automatic ones it is in fact your only chance to change the effective settings. Exposure Compensation is usually available in increments of one third of an Exposure Value. That's the value that the metering decides is required for a correct exposure, and that the shutter speed an aperture setting combine to create. It's easy to use though. If your photo is underexposed or too dark, it needs more light, so dial in +1/3rd, +2/3rd or even +1EV and retake exactly the same shot. If the photo is overexposed or too bright, then dial in a negative number for less light. Most cameras can manage plus or minus 1.5 or 2EV which should cover most circumstances.

Electronic Flash

Flash is that very brief, but ultra-bright burst of light that turns gloomy into sunny, night into day and banishes all color casts. It can freeze motion and produce creative effects. Any digital camera worth having, and plenty that aren't, have a built in flash system. In terms of creative usefulness and power they increase in that order. However, the most basic flash is built into the camera and is directly controlled by it. If your camera is on auto then the flash will automatically pop up when required, but if it is turned off then consider using it when the shutter speed drops below 1/15th of a second because otherwise camera shake will ensue.

The main problem with general use of flash is what is termed red eye. This occurs when the flash of light fires directly from the camera to the subject and illuminates the blood vessels at the back of the eye. The camera records it as a giant red globe taking up most of the iris. Many cameras come with red eye reduction mode which works to a degree by firing a series of spikes at the targets eye's to make the pupils contrast and so minimize the red eye effect. If your camera has it and you want to take photos of people, then activate the setting on your camera.

One of the most useful flash options available is fill-in flash for portraits. This is best used when there are deep shadows on the face. It works because the flash is weaker than ambient light so it fills in shadows but doesn't affect the rest of the face because the daylight there is brighter than the flash.

It's so useful that many DSLRs will use fill-flash as the default flash mode.

The main problem with the direct use of flash that isn't fill-flash, specifically at full power, is that it tends to flatten the scene, can be harsh and introduce unwanted shadows. If possible, it is better to use a tripod and slower shutter speeds, or a higher ISO rating than full on flash. More sophisticated options for using flash include having a slow synch or second curtain mode. In this the flash fires at the end of the exposure, rather than the beginning, leading to some creative effects where the rest of the scene is recorded in blurry fashion and then comes into sharp detail when the flash goes off.

The advantage of using a flashgun that sits on the camera hotshot (these are usually on DSLRs) is that it is further away from the lens and thus reduces or removes the red eye effect. You can also fit diffusers or other effects driven filters over the actual flash head for more creative or sophisticated flash use. Some hotshoe mounted flash can also be moved up and down to avoid directly hitting the target.

System flash is an extension of this, removing completely the red eye effect, giving more creative control, greater power and more directional control as well. It's still controlled by the camera so is easy to use. This is more expensive.

The system flash sits off to the side of the camera and is connected by a short cable. The ultimate flash system is studio flash, which requires the use of a light meter to work out the exposure for the camera because the camera triggers it, not controls it. This offers the greatest power and creative control, but is obviously tied to a studio or a portable mains generating power source.

CONCLUSION

When venturing into professional photography, you not only have to learn how to take the photographs right but also invest time into choosing the right tools for the job. With digital photography, every shot, every magnification power, and most definitely all the lighting matters. To some people, choosing the right camera could be as simple as throwing lot with a reputable manufacturer. To others, there is a clear distinction in what different cameras on a specific range could do.

Moreover, understanding that digital photography is never about presenting the photo as you captured it will give you an upper hand in the market. Learning how to use editing tools to smoothen out those pimples and make the skin glow will make your portrait photos come to live. Knowing how to use Photoshop in enhancing the blur on a nature photo shoot will make that lion or tiger seem like it is about to pounce out of the frame and share a vigorous hug.

www.ingramcontent.com/pod-product-compliance
Lightning Source LLC
Chambersburg PA
CBHW060404190526
45169CB00002B/740